THE COUNTRY LAWYER

Essays in Democracy

By

F. Lyman Windolph

Foreword by
Owen J. Roberts

UNIVERSITY OF PENNSYLVANIA PRESS

Philadelphia

1938

Manufactured in the United States of America
by the Lancaster Press, Inc., Lancaster, Pa.

London
Humphrey Milford
Oxford University Press

For permission to reprint certain chapters in this volume acknowledgment is made to *The Atlantic Monthly; The Forum; The Annals of the American Academy of Political and Social Science;* and *The Review.*

FOREWORD

EACH of the following essays, irrespective of its setting as one of the series, is of intrinsic interest. Those which describe the country lawyer's experiences are marked by ease and naturalness; those which present the author's views on legal and political questions are clear in method and forceful in statement; the remaining three have all the literary grace of the occasional essay at its best.

The collection is appropriately entitled *The Country Lawyer*. Its perusal well may engender in the metropolitan lawyer a sense of values lost by immersion in the more intense and narrowing activities of a city practice. If demonstration were needed that the country lawyer's way of life is the good way, here is the proof. The essays progressively present different aspects of this way of life, and form a satisfying and convincing composite picture.

The country lawyer's intimate contacts with all sorts and conditions of men in the vicissitudes of life, great and small, afford him a knowledge of human nature, ordinarily denied to his professional brother of the metropolis; and the close relation he maintains with all the human instruments of justice—fellow lawyers, judges, and jurors—is alien to the practice in a great city.

These form the raw material from which the country lawyer constructs his philosophy of life. To them is added leisure for reflection and synthesis; leisure, also, for the amenities of culture. In the successive chapters the author gives us not only the raw material, but offers the fruits of his use of it in thoughtful and challenging conclusions on matters professional, political, personal, and literary.

Thus he illustrates and portrays in its fullness the good life of the country lawyer, as he has lived it. The book should persuade ambitious youth that the country lawyer's rôle holds out possibilities of a rich and useful and happy career. Moreover, there is implicit the truth, which it is to be hoped the author will some time elaborate, that the country lawyer enjoys an unrivaled opportunity for service, and not merely as guide, counselor, and friend to his neighbors individually, but also as a civic leader in bettering the social and political conditions in his own community.

OWEN J. ROBERTS

Kimberton, Pa.,
July 25, 1938

CONTENTS

I

THE COUNTRY LAWYER

I CAME to the bar more than twenty-five years ago in the small American city near which I was born and in which I was brought up and educated. It had then a population of less than fifty thousand, but it was the center of a rich agricultural county so bounded by hills and by a great river as to form a naturally distinct geographical and political unit. The county had been settled half a century before the Revolution, and had existed as a separate judicial district for almost a century. In its courts James Buchanan, Thaddeus Stevens, and a score of other great lawyers had practised, and at the time of my admission to practice there were members of its bar who not only remembered the giants of other days but who had shared in and were able to transmit a legal tradition which stretched unbroken to 1729. In this community I have passed the whole of my professional life. In the course of it I have perforce written deeds and wills, organized corporations and issued bonds, settled estates and searched titles, and tried every sort of civil action from replevin to divorce and every sort of criminal case from assault and battery to murder. I have, in short, for better or worse lived the life of what the profession knows as a country lawyer.

Now the true test of the country lawyer is not the size or importance of the community in which he does his work, but rather the sort of work which he does and the sort of people for whom he does it. Some years ago I met a member of the bar of New York who was employed by a society engaged solely in the apprehension and prosecution of men who had married and deserted Jewish women. From year's end to year's end he traveled from place to place trying desertion cases, and I venture to say that he knew more at first hand about the comparative law of desertion throughout the United

States than any authority living. Such a man is obviously not a country lawyer, no matter where he may practise. On the other hand I remember with pleasure a conversation which I had not long ago with an old man who had practised for almost half a century in a remote county, whose largest town has less than three thousand inhabitants. In the course of our conversation he referred to himself as a country lawyer, and a moment afterward, in making some reference to me, made it clear that he regarded me as exactly the opposite. I think, however, that he was mistaken. If a lawyer performs every sort of legal service for every sort of client—the poor and the lowly as well as the rich and the well born—he is, within my definition at least, a country lawyer, and no arbitrary distinction based on density of population or the like can make him anything else.

Every sort of legal service for every sort of client—the very phrase brings to my mind a succession of pictures, some of them amusing, some of them tinged with sadness and tragedy, and some of them altogether gracious and lovely. There are memories, such as must come to every lawyer, of the routine of consultations and settlements, of trials by jury and hearings before magistrates, of wills made *in extremis*, and secret sorrows and disgraces unknown to the world at large. There are likewise memories—no less clear, but less directly connected with the law—of long drives to sales, a legal brother beside me in a buggy hired at a livery stable, and of cheerful talk about men and books as our horse jogged through the quiet countryside; of the sales themselves, with half a township as witnesses if not as bidders, the voice of the auctioneer rising and falling, and his chosen clerk keeping a record of purchases and making change with miraculous efficiency;[1] of road views, where a

[1] At a sale of personal property in the country, the clerk will sometimes, between noon and sundown, record the sale of eight hundred items, posting his entries as he goes, and will collect the total of the successful bids in cash without a discrepancy of so much as a penny. This is, however, an exceptionally hard afternoon's work.

keg of beer was as essential a part of the proceedings as the presence of the viewers themselves; and of a score of other aspects and incidents of rural civilization, some of which have passed away never to return, during the term of my own practice.

Of these recollections there is none which gives me greater pleasure than that of the country surveyor at work. Ordinarily there is no reason why a lawyer should be present at the making of a survey, but on one or two occasions some real or anticipated dispute about the meaning or effect of a deed has made it desirable that I should actually see the lines run on the ground. Now all our land titles are founded upon grants from the original proprietor, and just as, in Eastern mythology, the world rests upon the back of an elephant which in turn stands upon a turtle, so the proprietor obtained his title from King Charles II. It is as much a piece of impertinence to ask the source of the King's title as to inquire what the turtle stands on. Of course not every piece of land may actually be traced to the original proprietor, on account of lost deeds or the like, but many of them may. I am familiar with one tract, oddly enough a small one, whose present description is precisely the same as that contained in the first grant.

The running of boundary lines necessarily depends upon the location of landmarks, and the true worth of a country surveyor depends much less upon his skill with a transit than upon the accuracy of his information—necessarily acquired either by personal experience or by tradition—as to where these landmarks are to be found. The deeds refer to them only in general terms—"beginning at a white oak, a corner of lands of John Doe," thence by a certain course so many perches to "a stone," thence to "an iron pin," or to "a black oak," and so on. With such a description, a city-bred surveyor, however expert he may be, is as helpless in the setting of a disputed fence as a lawyer. I have stood on a wooded hillside looking for a stone—such a stone as might seem to serve as a monument—but seeing only white oaks (disturbingly numerous) and feeling only a sense of the futility of learning. Confronted by such a problem, the country surveyor lays aside for a moment the calling in which he is perhaps compelled to earn the greater part of his livelihood, and, not without a proper consciousness of the burden of responsibility resting upon him, comes grandly into his own. The question involved is rather of fact than of law, and its solution depends upon knowledge possessed by him alone. Surely there is nothing finer than the air with which, ignoring suggestions, he strides—it would be a slander to say jumps—into a bramble bush and scratches out, not his eyes, but the very stone which was pointed out to him by his grandfather, also a surveyor, half a century before.

On the witness stand in a courtroom he is a far less satisfying figure than on his native hills, because, all things being equal, erudition is always less satisfying than knowledge. In the country his worth and skill are self-demonstrating—the event itself speaks. But before a judge and jury he must justify himself and his profession in words, and he feels that in order to do so he must be given an opportunity by the lawyer who calls him as a witness to explain the variations in the magnetic compass. This is a mysterious subject, whose relation to the actual practice of surveying may, for all I know, be slight or none, but every country surveyor expects to have his qualifications as an expert tested in court by being interrogated about it. The question is no sooner on the lips of counsel than the answer is ready. In the year 1700 the magnetic compass pointed five degrees to the west of the true geographical north. Between 1700 and 1800 it moved four degrees to the eastward and so on. I doubt whether any respectable number of jurors have been much enlightened by the recital, but a disappointed witness sometimes means in the end a disappointed client, and five minutes devoted to the eccentricities of the compass are not too big a price to pay in order to put a witness at his ease.

It has been said that the trial of cases is the culmination of the lawyer's art. In the matter of dramatic intensity and interest, murder cases, as much in the country as elsewhere, are in a class by themselves. It is true that before country judges the point at issue is, as a rule—whether wisely or not—tried much more strictly than in the big cities and that witnesses are more rarely permitted to unfold in their testimony the entire stories of their lives. In my own county I am satisfied that the trial of Thaw, for example, would not have lasted at the most more than three days. It is likewise true that juries in murder cases are secured much more rapidly in the country than in cities. The original theory of trial by jury was that an accused person ought to be tried by a jury selected from his vicinage or neighborhood, because the jurors, being his neighbors, would be likely on that account to know something about him at first hand. Some tradition of this theory has persisted in the country, so that an intimate and detailed examination of prospective jurors with a view to uncovering some possible bias is not ordinarily permitted. Indeed—and apart from any theory—it would be impossible in many rural jurisdictions to secure twelve citizens who, if the defendant was a native of their county, did not know him or at least know something about him.

But making due allowance for the incidental differences in practice which tend to make a murder trial in the country less sensational than elsewhere, the essentials of legal solemnity and human interest necessarily remain. In my state the formal arraignment of the accused has been abolished in all cases except trials for murder and there is a strangeness, as of another age, in hearing the clerk ask the prisoner how he will be tried and in hearing the prisoner, usually prompted by his counsel, reply, "By God and my country." Then, too, the selection of a jury, though never a question be asked by the attorneys on either side, presents to the prisoner and his counsel a series of decisions on which life and death literally depend, and each of which seems more momentous than the last until only the twelfth juror remains to be chosen. The prospective juryman, on his name being called, presents himself at the entrance to the jury box. The clerk, standing facing him, asks the three time-honored questions—whether he has such conscientious scruples as would prevent him from rendering a verdict of guilty of murder in the first degree, the penalty being death, if the evidence should warrant the same; [2] whether he has formed such an opinion as would prevent him from rendering a verdict in accordance with the evidence; and whether he can be perfectly impartial between the Commonwealth and the prisoner. If the answers of the juror do not disqualify him, the clerk then says, "Juror, look upon the prisoner. Prisoner, look upon the juror. How say you, challenged or not challenged?" If the prisoner's attorney knows his business and has had reasonably good luck, a few, though perhaps a very few, of his original twenty peremptory challenges remain. There is a tense moment during which he consults his jury list or engages in a whispered colloquy with his client. If the juror comes from the regular panel, counsel for the defense probably knows something about him, but if there has been a special venire, as usually happens before the twelfth juror has been selected in a murder case, there is nothing to do except to judge by appearances and be governed accordingly. Old practitioners will tell you that in such cases butchers, carpenters, and all those who habitually handle edged tools are to be avoided. However kindly they

[2] As the result of a comparatively recent statute, the jury, if it finds the defendant guilty of murder in the first degree, must determine whether the penalty shall be death or imprisonment for life, and the clerk now says, "the penalty for which may be death," instead of "the penalty being death."

may be personally, they will bring in verdicts of murder in the first degree more readily than other men. The juror looks about him, uncertain whether to walk into the jury box or to return to his seat. Though the other eleven jurors would vote to acquit, this man may persuade them to find a verdict of guilty. On the other hand, his voice alone may save the defendant. Everything seems to depend upon him. "Pass the juror," says counsel for the accused. The judge looks up quickly and clears his throat. There is a long sigh from the spectators. The trial is ready to begin.

If the trial of cases is, for those who participate in it, a universal experience wherever the jury system is in force, there are other activities of the country lawyer which have no parallel in the practice of his brothers in the large cities. There is, for instance, the work of conveyancing—an art which is inextricably connected in my mind with a local custom known as "the first of April rush." It is said that the date was determined in the first place by the fact that tobacco—which for time out of mind has been one of our principal crops—was invariably paid for in the spring; but be that as it may, the custom itself resulted from the existence of a state of society sufficiently simple to permit a farmer to transact the whole of his annual worldly business, other than farming, between the morning and evening of a single day. From one April to another he lived entirely upon credit, paying no bills and expecting none to be paid. On the first of every April, rain or shine, he went to the county seat, and having established himself at a hotel, called upon his banker and withdrew enough money to meet his needs. Sometimes, indeed, he withdrew his entire balance in order to assure himself that it had been safely kept, and, because of the crowd within, counted it sitting on the curb in front of the bank. When his financial arrangements had been completed, he set about meeting his debtors and creditors, seeking them at the offices wisdom than I possess, but he answered only that he was considering buying a new plough, and that he wanted to know what I thought about it.

Now I am unfortunately blessed with no knowledge whatever about farming, but we had, nevertheless, an unhurried talk for perhaps ten minutes about farming in general and ploughs in particular. In the end we decided to buy the plough. I went to the outer door with my friend and said good-bye to him there, intending to return to my desk. The stenographers had left for the day and the office was empty. Suddenly I realized that I was very tired and that it was time to stop work. I got my hat, locked the door, and walked out into the April twilight with wet eyes.

Four ducks on a pond,
A grass-bank beyond,
A blue sky of spring,
White clouds on the wing:
What a little thing
To remember for years—
To remember with tears.

I will not say that one who is not touched and humbled by such an incident as this is a bad man, but I think that he will never be entirely happy or successful as a country lawyer. A measure of compensation for small fees and for the lack of great causes is to be found in that sense of legal totality which comes from a general practice. There is a picture—surely familiar to every lawyer who studied for his profession in the office of a preceptor—which shows the law as a gigantic tree, its roots buried in the common earth and its top reaching to the heavens. From its trunk grow the alternating branches of property and persons, of contracts and torts, of crimes, remedies, and government. The subject of equity is reduced to a small limb and bankruptcy to an even smaller one, while injunctions appear as a twig no thicker than the stem of a leaf.

I like to think that at one time or another I have perched on almost every limb of that tree.

But the chief compensation of the country lawyer is the richness of his share in the heritage which belongs of right to all the members of the three learned professions. Doubtless in the old sense there are no longer any learned professions. The architect, the engineer, the journalist, the scientist, and a hundred others have, indeed, fed as well upon learning as the physician, the lawyer, and the divine, but the old magic authority of learning—the old faith that education necessarily, or at least presumably, brings wisdom and goodness to its possessor—is as dead as that benefit of clergy which once served, with whatever injustice, to express it. And yet, because the great experiences of men are still births and deaths, their great concerns health, liberty, and happiness, and their great aim salvation, the three learned professions remain as obviously as ever in a place apart. After all, learning was never more than one of their incidental distinctions. Now as always their true distinction lies less in their achievements than in their purposes and in the resulting intimacy and beauty of those human relationships which occur so frequently in the life of the country lawyer. Whether or not his training has made him learned, his experience ought to make him wise and good.

It is not true that only God can make a tree. The Devil could make a tree if he tried, but only God can make men and women. With all of them we stand in jeopardy, and by some of them, it seems to me, He saves us every hour.

II
KING STREET

Ibam forte Via Sacra, sicut meus est mos,
Nescio quid meditans nugarum. . . .
Horace, *Sat.* I. 9.

King Street is the main street of the city in which I live. The city lies today, as when Kipling's Red Jacket visited it, in "a kindly, softly country there, back of Philadelphia"—so far back, indeed, that it has been from its foundation the center of an independent community and has recently celebrated the two-hundredth anniversary of its elevation to the dignity of a county seat. History will tell you that it was once the largest inland city in the United States, and that when the frightened Continental Congress fled westward after the battle of Brandywine it became for a few hours the capital of the United States, but these glories—if glories they were—have long since departed. Though every census has recorded its steady growth, it is a small city now.

Since I was born in the county over which it presides, I may call it my own city by an unimpeachable title which, however, suffers somewhat in dignity because of the fact that three of my four grandparents were born elsewhere. Anything less than title by birth is, as we reckon such matters, no title at all. Not long ago, in the heat of a political campaign, we were earnestly exhorted not to let "outsiders" tell us how to run our city, though of the two denizens—I will not be so unkind as to say aliens—thus held up to public suspicion one had lived among us for more than a quarter of a century and the other for at least half of that period.

So it comes about that my ancestral memories are perhaps less vivid and authentic than they would be if more of my progenitors had been to the manor born. I may not, for instance, speak of historical matters with the authority of my tobacconist, who conducts his business on the very site on which his great-great-great-grandfather established it in 1770. Though I attended the college that Benjamin Franklin helped to found, I can throw no light on the solution of the once mooted question whether he was personally present when the corner stone was laid. I remember the stagecoaches lumbering into King Street over the old stone bridge across the Conestoga River, but not the Conestoga wagons in the days of the Oregon Trail. I was born in the house once occupied by Baron Stiegel on the farms which he named Elizabeth, after his wife, but no echo comes to me of the salutes he caused to be fired from a neighboring hill (called Cannon Hill to this day) to welcome him home at the end of his journeys.

One of the Baron's neighbors, by the way, was a manufacturer of iron and a mighty hunter as well. One day, enraged at his failure in the chase and being deep in his cups, he drove his pack of foxhounds into the fire of one of his furnaces and burned them alive. The last to go through the door of the furnace was his favorite white bitch. She fawned upon him and cried piteously, begging to be spared, but he forced her remorselessly into the flames. Men say that on winter nights she still gives tongue, and that as often as she does so it is the doom of her cruel master to rise from his grave and follow her over the frozen hills of our northern townships. I too have heard strange sounds on winter nights, but I cannot certainly affirm that they came from the throat of the white bitch.

Let our legends be what they will. I am less concerned to recount hearsay than, like Mark Antony, "to speak what I do know." In order to do so I must confine myself to the last decade of the old century and the first of the new one —in which I grew up, went to school and college, and studied law—and to the years since then, in which I have been continuously engaged in the practice of my profession.

About three months after my graduation from college I began to study law, or, as our rules of court express it, to "serve a regular clerkship in the office of a practising attorney." It is almost impossible to assert that this is a bad way to study law, since, for want of a different one, it is the way in which all the lawyers of America received their legal education up to comparatively recent times. On the contrary, given the atmosphere of an old-fashioned law office, a preceptor with the time and ability to transmit to his student the fruits of his own experience, and a student not too easily discouraged by the absence of the stimulus that comes from competition and discussion with other students, I think it is an excellent way to study law. It has passed away utterly in the large cities and is passing away in my own city as well, because the circumstances which made it possible have in large measure ceased to exist. The fee to be paid by a student for his tuition was in my day, and still is, fixed by tradition at two hundred dollars, one half payable upon registration and the other half upon admission to the bar. As Thaddeus Stevens, whose office was popular with law students, is said to have remarked: "Some pay; some don't." I paid the whole of my fee a year or two after I had begun practice. No one ever asked me for the money.

A student in a law office has no rights that anyone is bound to respect. In times long past he was expected to sweep out the office and to attend to the stove in the winter, but I had no such tasks to perform. I searched titles, wrote deeds and mortgages, copied wills and other legal papers, and spent much time in court listening to the leaders of the bar of that day, the most famous of whom was an ex-attorney-general of Pennsylvania, whose former partner, then a member of the state Supreme Court, was afterwards its Chief Justice. In addition I learned to know a number of local characters directly or indirectly connected with the administration of justice.

There was a woman—for whom, as it now seems to me, something might have been done—who suffered from the delusion that she had a case which was just about to come up and who sat in court from the beginning to the end of every session waiting for her case to be called. There was a freckled colored man named Sam, a bootblack, who went the rounds of the law offices every morning, plying his trade and retailing the gossip of the day. There was an eccentric lawyer of morose appearance but consistently convivial habits, a strange mixture of Dr. Johnson and Boswell—given like the former to sudden and startling ejaculations, and like the latter to the making of minute written records of casual conversations. I once heard him begin an argument in the Orphans' Court about the distribution of the estate of a man named Grimes by remarking in a resonant voice, "If Your Honor please, old Grimes is dead." For all his eccentricities, he was a careful and competent lawyer, scrupulously exact in the transaction of his professional business, and as methodical in his personal habits as one of his predecessors at the bar—whom I never knew, but of whom I have often heard—who was accustomed to shave every other day, and who attended divine service only on those alternate Sundays when the calendar brought the rite of shaving into proper conjunction with the rites of the church.

The simplest and most rudimentary act of a lawyer is to hang up a sign and sit down to wait for his first client. Every lawyer who has done so—and who has exercised the self-denial, endured the disappointments and been rewarded by the satisfactions which ordinarily belong to that experience—will come to feel toward the practice which he afterwards acquires something of the sense of wonder with which Darius

Clayhanger in Arnold Bennett's massive novel of that name regarded the business of his printing establishment.

> Darius's pride in the achievement of his business was simply indescribable. . . . How had he done it? He did not know. Certainly he did not credit himself with brilliant faculties. He knew he was not brilliant; he knew that once or twice he had had luck. . . . To Darius there was no business quite like his own. He admitted that there were businesses much bigger but they lacked the miraculous quality that his own had. They were not sacred. His was, genuinely. Once, in his triumphant and vain early manhood he had had a fancy for bull-dogs; he had bred bull-dogs; and one day he had sacrificed that great delight at the call of his business; and now no one could guess that he knew the difference between a setter and a mastiff!

The Greeks said truly that you become a carpenter by doing carpenter's work. In like manner you become a trial lawyer by trying cases. It is almost in the spirit of Darius Clayhanger that I think of the trial of my first case before a court and jury.

The case arose from a dispute in connection with the sale of a crop of tobacco. The ostensible plaintiff was the owner of the farm on which the tobacco had been grown, but the real party in interest was his son, a young man of about my own age who had cared for the tobacco without help from anyone and whose entire compensation for a year's work on his father's farm was represented by the price which the tobacco would bring. A few days in advance of the trial I went over the case carefully with all of our witnesses. At the conclusion of my examination the father said, "You are a young man. Do you think you are fit to try this case alone?" I answered that I thought I was, and waited for what seemed to me the inevitable additional question as to how many other cases I had tried. He said nothing further, however, and we went to trial.

The contract between the seller and buyer had provided that the tobacco was to be of merchantable quality and the defense was that it did not conform to this description. I am inclined to think that the experienced and busy lawyer who represented the defendant had not prepared his case with very great care. At all events he put on the stand among other witnesses a tobacco buyer who had seen the tobacco on its way to delivery at the defendant's warehouse, and asked him what the quality of the tobacco was. "Well," answered the witness, "it was not the kind of tobacco I was buying." The presiding judge turned in his chair. "That is not the question," he said, "was it merchantable?" The witness hesitated. "Yes," he answered at length, "I think it was merchantable." If I had been more experienced I would have known that for all practical purposes the case was over at that point. I did not know it, but I had enough sense not to cross-examine the witness.

A day or two after the verdict had been rendered I chanced to meet one of the jurors, a retired blacksmith who had worked for many years in the blacksmith shop at the bridge across the Conestoga. I had known him all my life and as a matter of course we shook hands. I expected that he would congratulate me at once on the skill and address with which I had handled the tobacco case. Instead he talked for some minutes about indifferent matters. Finally he said, "That was a very easy case you had. Anybody could have won that case, and it did not take us long to decide it." Across the lapse of more than a quarter of a century I can see that he was quite right, but at the time it seemed to me that he was sadly lacking in appreciation. My client was more generous. On the day on which the verdict was paid I settled my accounts with him and received from him the fee to which I was entitled. "I was a little afraid about you at first," he said, "but you did all right." As soon as he had left me, I went into the tobacco shop on King Street and with a part of the fee bought a pipe on which I had had my eye for a long time. It is still the best pipe I have and I would not part with it for a good deal.

The *dramatis personae* of a small community are infinitely various. In addition, they acquire a semi-official standing and a local universality of influence which have no counterparts in a really large city, except perhaps in the lives of the notorious figures of its underworld. The reason lies in the very nature of provincial civilization. A lawyer or a musician living, for example, in London or New York may, if he chooses, so order his affairs as to spend all of his leisure hours in the company of those interested in the work in which he is engaged or engaged in similar work of their own, but the resident of a small city can of necessity make no such selection of his acquaintances. For better or worse, he must reckon with the whole of a small environment rather than with a selected portion of a large one. He must, in short, accept the common lot of social interdependence, and, as Mr. Chesterton has somewhere pointed out, live a broad life at the inevitable risk of living a shallow one.

Breadth and depth are, after all, relative terms. When used in a figurative sense they are inaccurate as well. Our most influential citizen during the early years of my practice was the minister of one of our local churches—a small, frail man without physical distinction of any sort—who was probably unheard of outside the limits of the city in which he lived and worked. I remember having heard my mother say that in her youth she thought him a little mad because of the perfect simplicity with which he bowed to everyone he met, whether he knew the person or not. He was not a modern man. I think he lived and died happy, but he would have been happier still if he had been born in the great days of the thirteenth century. He was the only person I have ever known who spoke naturally in the language of Saint Francis' "Canticle to the Sun."

The truth is that I did not really know him. I saw him hundreds of times, but I have no recollection of having ever addressed him except once, and then only by making a written inquiry as to a date shown in the baptismal records of his parish. He answered me in longhand by the next post, thanking me at the outset for my "good letter" and giving me the information requested. As a matter of fact, my letter was in no way different from any other formally worded inquiry. Doubtless he did not stop to reason about the matter, but I think nevertheless that he did not call it good merely as the result of a literary habit. It was a letter from a man, and therefore his instinct was to regard it as a good letter. At bottom he cared more about people than about ideas.

He cared more about charity than about efficiency. I am sure that he gave his support to all the organized efforts for social welfare that were made in his day—to the ministerial associations, the community-service associations, and the law-and-order societies. He would no more have thought of opposing the work of such organizations than of opposing the work of the fire department. It is better to damage property with water than to let fires burn, and it is better for society to put prostitutes in jail than to have them walking the streets. But in his heart he had no interest in abstract conceptions like society. He knew a good many prostitutes, although I am not sure that he realized the business in which they were engaged. If he had realized it, I do not know what he would have done. It might have been something as irrelevant as to stoop down and with his finger write on the ground.

If the members of provincial society are more dependent than others in their personal relationships, they are far more independent than others in their attitude toward the law and the problems with which the law is concerned. A whole chapter of legal history is suggested in the contrast. The times have passed when drunkenness was regarded as an aggravation of a crime committed, and when every citizen boasted of his right to bear arms. In these instances we have all turned about face—drunkenness, though we have sought by statute to prevent it altogether, may now be pleaded everywhere as a defense to crime, and the trend of modern legislation is to forbid the bearing of arms without a license from the police. There are, however, other connections in which the older tradition of independence and responsibility persists. A man may still lawfully strike in his own defense, eject trespassers from his real estate, retake his stolen goods, and abate nuisances, but it is only in the country that such rights amount to anything in practice—it is only in the country that one may still watch the erection of a "spite fence" or observe the discomfiture of a telephone company whose employees come to set a pole in a prepared hole and find the hole occupied by a heroic, sturdy old lady who refuses to budge.

The spite fence with which I am most familiar is not really a fence at all. It was constructed by a client of mine who had no actual spite in her heart, but who acted, as she thought, defensively; and it is in its way a masterpiece of ingenuity. The client in question, an unmarried woman of middle age, lived alone in a small house which had belonged to her parents and in which she had been brought up. She spent most of her leisure time in the kitchen, which opened to the south on a small and pleasant garden. When, in course of time, the property on the south changed hands and her new neighbor, who was a barber, began to construct a window looking directly into her garden and kitchen, she was outraged beyond measure. Her sense of outrage lay principally in a feeling that she was being imposed upon because she was a woman, and that if she had had "a man in the house" no one would have dared to disturb her privacy. I purposely said nothing to her about obstructing the window, telling her simply that her neighbor was entirely within his rights, that he probably felt a need for additional light and air, and that there was no reason to suppose that he wanted to spy upon her.

A week or two passed; the offending window was completed and proved unendurable. She arrived in her own mind at the idea of shutting it and called to her aid a sympathetic plumber, who was both an architect and an artificer. Together they sank in concrete two pipes, to the tops of which they screwed a steel plate exactly the size of the window. The window was on the property line and the plate shut it as effectively as a lid shuts a box.

Within a few days I received a call from the barber, who, as I suspect, had previously consulted his own attorney and had been advised that he was without a legal remedy. It was summer, and he complained that the steel plate cast heat into his house in such a way as to make life unendurable for himself and family. I explained to him that I regretted his inconvenience, but that there was nothing I could do to help him. At parting he said, "You tell that woman to take that plate down or I will paint my house red, white, and blue, in stripes." This threat was duly transmitted to his antagonist, but she remained inflexible. It was the barber's last move. He never carried out his patriotic idea about the painting. Years have passed and I do not know whether or not he has moved away. I do know, however, that the plate remains triumphantly in place.

Much has been written recently about life in villages and small cities in the United States, and the composite picture presented is, to say the least, an unpleasant one. I think it might well be argued that this picture is false. If a philosopher were to make a list of the things men in the abstract would say were best worth living for—friendship, leisure, beauty, quiet—it is certainly not in the big cities that he would find them. There is, moreover, a certain charm in small communities—in the definiteness and finality of their social categories, in the simplicity of their human relationships, most of all in the genuineness of the interest which their members feel toward one another—which springs perhaps from the qualities of those very defects which have been so much in the public eye. It has been said that there are two words for everything, the word that swells and the word that belittles. Perhaps the swelling words in this particular connection are those which have remained unwritten.

But I am not a philosopher, and I have no wish to do anything so dreary as to engage in a debate on the relative merits of rural and urban civilization. Still less do I wish to set up the proposition that life in small cities is stupid, narrow, and ugly, and then to rebut it, as one rebuts the proposition that all crows are black by producing one white crow. There are, God knows, enough evil things in every community, big or little, to give pause to the most ardent local patriot about to cast the first stone. I mean to do no more than to bear testimony to some of the characteristics of life in the small city with which I happen to be best acquainted. The testimony is true. I cannot speak for Main Street, but King Street is at all events a real street in a real city.

If you're off to Philadelphia this morning,
And wish to prove the truth of what I say,
I pledge my word you'll find the pleasant land behind
Unaltered since Red Jacket rode that way.
Still the pine woods scent the noon; still the catbird sings his tune;
Still autumn sets the maple forest blazing.
Still the grapevine through the dusk flings her soul-compelling musk;
Still the fire-flies in the corn make night amazing!
    They are there, there, there with Earth immortal,
    (Citizens, I give you friendly warning)
    The things that truly last when men and times have passed,
    They are all in Pennsylvania this morning.

III

COUNTRY JUSTICE

THERE is no need to quote authorities in order to convince the people of the United States that disregard of law constitutes one of the major problems with which the present generation is confronted, and that any intelligent inquiry as to how our laws may be better enforced necessarily involves a consideration of how the procedure of our criminal courts may be reformed.

That a reformation of this procedure is badly needed seems, indeed, to have been taken for granted by nearly everyone who has discussed the subject during the course of the last decade. The reforms suggested (or actually adopted in certain states) have been many and various. They include allowance of a conviction without proof of the defendant's guilt beyond a reasonable doubt, abolition of the rule forbidding comment on his failure to testify in his own behalf, a reduction in the number of the jury and abolition of the requirement of a unanimous verdict. Some of these innovations are comparatively unimportant, but in the aggregate they express a profound and growing distrust in trial by jury as a means of administering justice in criminal cases.

Now trial by jury is the most characteristic contribution which our race has made to the practical science of jurisprudence. On that account, if for no other reason, it ought not to be lightly discarded. It was in its origin essentially a rural instrumentality, and the interesting suggestion has been made on a number of occasions—notably by Dean Pound in the course of an address to the Judicial Section of the American Bar Association—that its present disrepute results very largely from the unsuccessful attempt to adapt it to the needs of an increasingly urban civilization. If this is so, it may be worth while to record the comments of a country lawyer on the trial procedure of courts in the large cities. Many of the matters usually included in the term "procedure" are so universal and rigid as to be incapable of being changed except by constitutional amendment. Others, however, are entirely local and flexible, and are governed by rules of court, which may be altered at pleasure, or merely by the customary practices of the courts in which they occur. If trial by jury works better today in the country than in the cities, perhaps it does so less in the nature of the case than because, for reasons not in themselves compelling, it is administered in the country more nearly than elsewhere in accordance with its own genius and traditions. Perhaps, in short, there has been too much adaptation instead of too little, and the trouble is not so much with the instrument as with the way in which the instrument has been used.

What most surprises a country lawyer about the trial of cases in large cities may be summed up in a single sentence. In most instances the practice followed seems extraordinarily wasteful of time. This comment is the more surprising because efficiency is on the whole preached with more fervor and practised with more consistency in the large cities than anywhere else. Indeed in every connection except the trial of cases the city lawyer sets a record of promptness which the country lawyer cannot hope to equal.

In the course of a general country practice I have been employed at various times to prepare mortgages intended to secure issues of corporate bonds. A mortgage of this sort is an elaborate legal document whose average length is perhaps thirty thousand words. If I were instructed tomorrow to prepare one, there would be descriptions to secure, forms to consult, and various alternate provisions, both as to the terms of the bonds and as to the remedies of the bondholders in case of default, to consider and pass upon. A large amount of typewriting would have to be done. After the copy had been given to the printer there would be proof to read and corrections to make. At the very least it would take me a week to have such a mortgage ready for execution, though there are law firms in New York which would undertake to do the same work in twenty-four hours. And yet a country judge and two country lawyers can dispose of a murder case in a number of days no greater than the number of weeks which would be required to dispose of it in any one of a dozen metropolitan jurisdictions.

I once made this point in the course of an after-dinner speech in the presence of one of the leading trial lawyers at the New York bar. In the course of his own speech, which followed mine, he said, "My friend doesn't know what practice in the country really is. He ought to move to [the middle-western state in which the speaker had begun his own practice]. *Out there they will try a case for four days for a fee of ten dollars.*" The remark struck me as significant because of its unconscious disregard of the point really involved. The speaker instinctively felt that it was a foolish thing to try a case for four days for a fee of ten dollars, though presumably not a foolish thing to try a case for forty days for a fee of, say, a thousand dollars a day. And yet it is to be observed that I had spoken—and that I am now writing—not about money but about time. Great gifts receive and deserve to receive a great reward. The testimony is unanimous, however, that four days is a long time in which to try a case in the country.

But indeed I do not mean to argue that the jury system is good because it is prompt, though promptness is conceded to be one of its outstanding merits even by those who are opposed to the system as a whole. I mean rather that where the jury system is not administered promptly it is not administered characteristically and therefore is not administered well. Moreover, I am not referring to delay in bringing cases to trial. The problem of the congested court calendar is one peculiar to the big cities, and much good work has been done in recent years in the effort to solve it. I am referring to delay occurring in the actual trial of cases and arising from causes which have no necessary connection with the differences between conditions in the country and in the cities.

Some of these causes were illustrated in the trial of George Remus for the murder of his wife, which took place in Cincinnati during the concluding months of the year 1927. The illustration is a good one because it would be difficult, if not impossible, to find a murder case in which the issues were less complicated. The killing was admitted and the only defense was insanity, the defendant contending that he had been insane at the time of the killing, but that he was sane at the time of the trial. Hypothetical questions were excluded, seemingly by agreement, and as I read the newspaper reports of the proceedings the testimony of all the alienists examined occupied only one day.

The defendant had killed his wife on October 6, 1927, and was called for trial on November 14 of the same year. (There can be no denial therefore that he was accorded a speedy trial. Not many rural jurisdictions can show an average record of greater promptness, and I doubt whether greater promptness is in general desirable.) On December 20 his case was submitted to the jury, which rendered a verdict of not guilty in nineteen minutes. Including the nineteen minutes, the trial occupied thirty actual days, the time not spent in court between the two dates named being represented by Sundays and one additional day on which the presiding judge (no doubt a loyal alumnus) went to see the Ohio State football team in action.

The first five of these thirty days were spent in selecting a jury. To a country lawyer this seems unreasonably long. Mr. Justice Riddell, Justice of Appeals of Ontario, Canada, in his interesting review of the Sacco-Vanzetti case, says that he never but once saw it take more than half an hour to obtain a jury in a murder case, and that on that one occasion it took forty-eight minutes. I am afraid that justice even in the rural parts of the United States is not quite so rapid as that of the Canadian variety, but it would be hard to convince an American country lawyer that there can be any good reason for spending more than a day at the most in the selection of a jury in any sort of case.

It appears that in Ohio the prosecution has four peremptory challenges in a murder case and the defense sixteen, though in a number of other states, my own included, each side has twenty. On the other hand, the practice followed in Ohio necessitates the selection of thirteen jurors—the thirteenth sitting as an emergency juror but taking no part in the decision of the case unless one of the other twelve is disqualified. As a matter of fact, however, the length of time required to obtain a jury does not depend to any great extent upon rules such as these, but upon the number and nature of the questions which counsel are permitted to ask prospective jurors. In my own jurisdiction the clerk of the court asks each juror three general questions—whether he has conscientious scruples against capital punishment; whether he has formed an opinion; and whether he can be impartial. I have occasionally heard counsel ask questions of their own—usually as to a possible relationship or intimacy with the accused or with witnesses who were to be called. I have never heard an examination intended to find out a juror's state of mind, in the abstract, toward the antecedents of the defendant or toward such a defense as he was likely to interpose. Moreover, I do not know what is meant by seating jurors tentatively. When we seat them we do so for all purposes, and there is no opportunity to revise the decision arrived at.

In the Remus case the defendant—who had formerly been a member of the bar and who took an active part in his own defense—was permitted to ask prospective jurors whether they would be prejudiced against him because he had (1) served a term in the federal prison at Atlanta, (2) testified before the Wheeler senate investigating committee at Washington, (3) testified in the Warden Sartain case at Atlanta, and (4) been involved in the Jack Daniels distillery case in Indianapolis and St. Louis. A juror in answer to questions like these said, "I do not favor bootleggers." One of the defendant's attorneys thereupon said, "You still have that prejudice against bootleggers, haven't you, Miss Thompson?" and counsel on the other side objected—it appears not because of the scope of the examination but because, as he put it, "Every law-abiding person is supposed to be prejudiced against crime and criminals." A little later on the defendant, acting on his own behalf, asked a juror whether the fact that Mr. Taft, who was one of the counsel for the prosecution, was a son of the Chief Justice of the United States would prejudice the juror in the trial of the case. The juror answered "No" and, turning to Mr. Taft, remarked, "Kind of funny how that is, that examination." A country lawyer thinks it is kind of funny too, but five days of it is too much.

It is too much not because time is of more importance than justice but because, in addition to wasting time, it puts justice in jeopardy. If the questions propounded were not entirely without relevancy, it is fair to assume that those jurors who, like Miss Thompson, did not "favor bootleggers" proved objectionable to the defendant, and that their fellows who lacked that prejudice against crime which, in the philosophy of counsel for the prosecution, every law-abiding person is supposed to have, proved equally objectionable to the prosecution. Presumably, therefore, the ideal juror was someone without any views whatever about the enforcement of the Eighteenth Amendment. As most of us remember, such Americans were not easy to find during the period in which the Amendment was in force. I suggest, moreover, that when found they were not likely to prove desirable jurors. Trial by jury does not presuppose a tribunal composed of twelve persons altogether devoid of ideas or even of prejudices. It does presuppose a tribunal of sufficient intelligence and courage to arrive in spite of prejudice at a just determination of the issues submitted to it.

Both during and after the selection of the jury in the Remus case additional delay arose from extended legal arguments, during at least three of which the jurors were removed from the courtroom. On one of these occasions the defendant had asked a juror whether the fact that he had been disbarred as a practicing attorney in the State of Illinois because of his conviction for violating the Volstead Act would be likely to prejudice the juror against him. Counsel for the prosecution said that they objected to the question because they knew other reasons why the defendant had been disbarred, and the jurors were taken from the room while the court was told what the other reasons were. In the course of the altercation that followed, the defendant said to one of the opposing counsel, "Man, if I had you in the corridor I would wreck you physically." A colleague of the threatened attorney replied, "Get back on your own side of the railing or I will take a crack at you."

It would be hard to show that the jury missed anything in being denied this particular piece of repartee, but it nevertheless seems to a country lawyer that the objection of counsel might well have been ruled on promptly and in the presence of the jurors. Indeed the practice of removing the jury during the discussion of questions of law is, so far as I know, almost unknown in the country. When such a question has arisen in the course of a trial I have sometimes seen the trial judge engage in a whispered colloquy with counsel for both parties before making his ruling. Less frequently I have seen a judge send out for a law book or adjourn a few minutes in advance of the usual hour in order to consult the authorities. The same legal points must certainly come up in one jurisdiction as in another. Most of them may be disposed of in advance of the trial by judgments entered on demurrers or motions to quash the indictment, or after the trial as the result of motions in arrest of judgment or for a new trial. New trials are unquestionably an evil, but I doubt whether an analysis of the reports of the various appellate courts would show that more convictions are reversed in appeals from rural jurisdictions than in appeals from the trial courts of large cities. I doubt in short whether elaborate arguments are more effective than brief ones in reducing errors in the admission and rejection of evidence.

Here again the loss of time involved is to be regarded as symptomatic of an ailment rather than as the ailment itself. A trial by jury is a drama which ought to move with as few interruptions as possible to its appointed close. A jury is an entirely casual body, called together for a single purpose and dismissed as soon as that purpose has been accomplished. It passes chiefly upon human veracity, and it does so not by the application of technical rules but in the light of common sense. A just verdict depends much less upon the learning and ability of the jurors than upon their maintenance of a certain emotional detachment in which the contentions of both parties as presented in the testimony may be considered and compared. Other things being equal, the shortest trial is always the best.

Moreover, the removal of a jury from the courtroom for hours and indeed sometimes for days at a time makes a very bad impression on the jurors themselves. I once exchanged letters about the merits of the jury system with a civil engineer, seemingly a highly intelligent man, who lived in Los Angeles. He complained that he had belonged to a peripatetic jury which had been led in and out of court half a dozen times without having been permitted to find out what the case in which it was sitting was about. His point was not so much that this procedure wasted his time and that of his fellows while the lawyers argued questions which would probably be re-argued in any event, as that the law treated jurors as if they were only quasi-competent—that is, incompetent to hear the whole story whether of fact or law—and he resented what he thought was an unfair reflection on his intelligence.

I am not sure that his attitude in this respect was entirely justifiable, but it serves to demonstrate that if a jury is to do its work well there must be a limit to the number of confusing interruptions to which its members are subjected. There must likewise be a limit to the amount of eloquence to which they are subjected. In the Remus case this eloquence lasted for almost three days. Cases differ so greatly in complexity that it is hazardous to say how much time ought to have been allowed for summations in a given instance, but I believe most country lawyers would agree with the general statement that no case can be closed more effectively than in speeches limited to an hour for each side. If the facts of a particular case make an hour inadequate, the alternatives presented are to leave something unsaid or to submit to jaded jurors instead of to fresh ones the evidence upon which alone their verdict ought to depend. The risk of a miscarriage of justice involved in the adoption of the first of these alternatives seems to me in every way smaller than that involved in the adoption of the second. If this is heresy against the traditions of forensic eloquence, I shall have to take the consequences. I am persuaded, however, that it is not heresy but sound doctrine. When one considers that a lecturer speaking to those who have voluntarily come to listen to him can rarely hold the attention of his audience for more than an hour, it must be obvious that under ordinary circumstances a lawyer cannot expect to hold for a longer period what is, in a sense at least, the involuntary attention of a jury.

But it may be said with truth that if we deduct the time spent in the Remus trial in the selection of a jury and in the closing addresses of counsel, there remain upwards of twenty days which were occupied with the taking of testimony. I have not said that the Remus case was badly tried, but only that it illustrated some of the practices which make justice less rapid and, as I view the matter, less certain in the courts of big cities than elsewhere. Perhaps, indeed, within certain standards of trial procedure it was excellently tried, but I venture to think nevertheless that the examination of the witnesses would have been completed in the country in less than the time which was actually required. This is so because the standard of trial procedure to which the average country judge conforms requires him to rule out as irrelevant much evidence which the average metropolitan judge would admit without question.

In order to test these conclusions it is not without interest to compare the Remus trial with the so-called "witchcraft cases" which were tried a little more than a year afterwards in the small city of York, Pennsylvania. The murdered man was one Nelson Rehmeyer, who lived alone in the country about fifteen miles from York. He was what is known as a "powwow doctor" and possessed among other treasures a book called *The Long Lost Friend*, which is a treatise on witchcraft and other occult practices. (I may say in passing that I am the owner of a copy of this book, and that if it confers upon its possessor a tithe of the virtues and powers which it professes to confer Rehmeyer must be regarded as having been a happy man.) During the latter part of the year 1928 a family named Hess, who also lived in York County, had lost numerous chickens from disease and theft. They concluded that someone had put a "spell" on them and employed another powwow doctor, whose name was Blymyer, to lift the spell. Blymyer stated that in order to do so he would have to have a lock of Rehmeyer's hair and the latter's copy of *The Long Lost Friend.* On the evening of November 27, 1928, Blymyer, Wilbert Hess (a son of the owner of the bewitched chickens) and a boy named Curry went to Rehmeyer's house in order to get the lock of hair and the book, and in the course of a struggle killed him.

Blymyer, Hess, and Curry were indicted for murder, and demanded separate trials, which under the laws of Pennsylvania they had a right to do. The right in question is purely statutory, and I doubt whether it is wisely accorded. At all events three successive trials were required, the first of which began on Monday, January 7, 1929. The time which elapsed between the murder and the trials was therefore a day or two longer than that which elapsed between the killing of Mrs. Remus and the arraignment of her husband. In two of the three cases the defense, as in the Remus case, was insanity. In the third case, the defendant denied having struck the deceased, and contended at least by implication that he had acted throughout under the domination of his two associates.

The three trials lasted exactly six days. In the case against Blymyer, which was tried first, three hours were required to select a jury. There were two closing speeches, each fifty minutes in length. The jury deliberated for two hours and rendered a verdict of guilty of murder in the first degree, with a penalty of imprisonment for life, at 7:30 o'clock on the evening of Wednesday, January 9. The trial of Curry began on the following morning at 9:30 o'clock, and a jury was obtained in one hour and ten minutes. At the conclusion of the testimony, counsel for the defendant addressed the jury for thirty minutes and counsel for the Commonwealth for forty minutes. The jury was out for two hours and fifty minutes, and brought in a verdict of guilty of murder in the first degree, with a penalty of imprisonment for life, at 1:42 p.m. on Friday, January 11. Hess was immediately called for trial. In this case the selection of a jury consumed two hours, the final speech of the defendant's attorney lasted for one hour and ten minutes, and the final speech of the District Attorney lasted for forty minutes. At 7:25 p.m. on Saturday, January 12, the jury, after a deliberation of two hours and fifteen minutes, rendered a verdict of guilty of murder in the second degree, the maximum penalty for which is imprisonment for twenty years.

The "witchcraft cases" would have proved a nine-days wonder to the press and public except for two important circumstances. In the first place—and as already pointed out—they did not last for nine days. In the second place the manner in which they were tried made it impossible for the press to convert them into a wonder of any sort. When the first trial began at least a hundred representatives of metropolitan newspapers were in court, and the public had been informed that a "witchcraft trial" without a precedent in a century was about to be held. The truth was, of course, that the subject of witchcraft was involved only to the extent that it had a bearing on the question of the sanity of the defendants and that the cases were not a whit more interesting or important than rural murder trials ordinarily are. The presiding judge refused to permit telegraphic instruments to be installed in the Court House, refused to be photographed, and excluded photographers from the courtroom. The defendants were represented by experienced trial lawyers. Their cases were presented to the jury in due course, but before the week was out most of the reporters had gone home. One of them afterwards wrote a magazine article commenting bitterly on the reception which he had received and contrasting it with his reception at a historical pageant which had been held in the same city a few months previously.

I must deal here with an objection which will instantly occur to almost every reader. Hunterdon County, New Jersey, is as definitely rural as York County, Pennsylvania, yet the trial of Bruno Richard Hauptmann, which took place at Flemington, Hunterdon County, in January and February of the year 1935 was not only long drawn out, but was conducted in an atmosphere of almost unparalleled sensation and sentiment. If I thought this objection were valid I might perhaps dismiss it by saying that the notoriety of the exception is sufficient proof of the existence of a contrary rule. In my opinion, however, at least a partial answer may be made on the merits.

In the first place the evidence in the Hauptmann case was both circumstantial and complicated. Both the prosecution and the defense were compelled to make use of expert witnesses, and much time was necessarily consumed in the examination and cross-examination of these experts. In addition, a number of adjournments were granted at the request of the defense on account of the absence of persons described as material witnesses.

Nevertheless, the entire trial—including the selection of a jury, the addresses of counsel, the charge of the court and the deliberations preceding the verdict—was completed in thirty-two actual days. In other words, though the issue in the Hauptmann case was beyond comparison more complex and difficult than that in the Remus case, the trial in Flemington occupied only two days more than the earlier trial in Cincinnati.

But in the second place, though Mr. Justice Trenchard, who presided in Flemington, may perhaps be described as a country judge, the lawyers in active charge of the Hauptmann case were not country lawyers. Mr. Sidney B. Whipple, in his recent and authoritative review of the case,[1] concludes that

[1] *The Trial of Bruno Richard Hauptmann*, Doubleday, Doran and Co., 1937.

the blame for the unseemly features of the trial rests squarely on "publicity-seeking lawyers" and principally on Edward J. Reilly of Brooklyn, the chief counsel for the defense. In Mr. Whipple's opinion,

> . . . the position [of Mr. Reilly] is worthy of some comment. His visits with his distinguished client were comparatively few. His "press" (because he was generous in words and promises) was comparatively large. Altogether he struck an incongruous note in the whole proceedings. Florid, expansive, and given to the type of histrionics that impresses the small, urban mind, he could not seem to realize that he was dealing with an entirely different kind of mentality. In Brooklyn he might berate and bully a police witness with impunity, because many a Brooklyn juror would enjoy seeing a policeman's importance deflated. But country folk have more respect for the police, whom they regard as a protective and not unkindly force. They were, in this case, decidedly unimpressed by the clothes, the manner or the arguments of Hauptmann's chief advocate.

I have not read all the testimony in any of the cases to which reference has been made. On that account my opinion as to the merits of the verdicts rendered is entitled to little weight. If I were pressed for an opinion I should have to say that the verdict in the Remus case seems to me to have been without justification and that the verdicts in the Hauptmann case and in two of the three witchcraft cases seem to me to have been abundantly justified. In the instance of Curry, who was only fourteen years of age, I think a conviction of murder in the first degree was probably too severe.[2] With these questions I am, however, not primarily concerned. I am comparing general practices, not particular results. The guilt or innocence of all of the defendants was, in accordance with our

[2] Curry's conviction was reduced by the State Board of Pardons from murder in the first degree to murder in the second degree. An application for his parole was subsequently refused. Hess's minimum sentence will expire in 1939 and he will no doubt be released at that time.

system of jurisprudence, for determination by the juries which tried them. The verdicts speak for themselves. Under any system of jurisprudence innocent men will sometimes be done to death and guilty men will sometimes go free. Moreover, no lawyer can be unmindful of the fact that though all of the verdicts were in accordance with the evidence, they were perhaps quite different from those larger determinations of guilt or innocence in which the law has no part and which, being founded upon knowledge, are without the need of evidence.

So much may be taken for granted. It may likewise be taken for granted that a question exists whether trial by jury in criminal cases ought to be retained. If, however, as seems likely, this question is to be answered in the affirmative, the reforms which are most needed are not to be accomplished by constitutional or statutory changes in the rights of accused persons or in the rules of evidence. They are procedural rather than structural. They depend upon lawyers and judges rather than upon laws and amendments, and upon customs rather than upon formal rules. The country lawyer and the country judge have much to learn from the city lawyer and the city judge, but they have something to teach in return. They speak and act in the authentic tradition of the methods and practices which caused our ancestors to write into the constitutions of the original states their conviction that trial by jury ought to remain as theretofore.

IV

DEFENDING A BAD CAUSE

ON SUNDAY, February 1, 1623, Archbishop Laud recorded in his diary that he had that day stood by the most illustrious Prince Charles Stuart, at dinner. The Prince "was then very merry, and talked occasionally of many things with his attendants. Among other things, he said that if he were necessitated to take any particular profession of life he could not be a lawyer, adding his reason: 'I cannot (saith he) defend a bad, nor yield in a good cause.' "

Twenty-six years afterward, almost to the day, the former Prince, then Charles I, was beheaded at Whitehall, though whether in a good or a bad cause—whether as a glorious martyr or an inglorious tyrant—is a question about which honorable and patriotic Englishmen contested with one another on the field of battle as well as in debate for more than a century after his death, and came at last to peace and a mutual toleration rather than to agreement.

The cause of King Charles has passed, never to be finally decided, into the realm of old, unhappy, far-off things. His theory of the divine right of kings is dead, but his opinion about the practice of law is as representative of the opinions of a large number of intelligent men and women today as it doubtless was when he made his casual statement of it on that Sunday morning three hundred years ago.

I have listened a score of times to informal discussions among laymen about the ethics of the legal profession. Sometimes no more is expressed than a mere personal disinclination to be a lawyer, as on the part of Prince Charles, because of the necessity of urging unconscionable claims and defenses. Sometimes a question is asked like that which Boswell addressed to Dr. Johnson: "But what do you think of supporting a cause which you know to be bad?" Sometimes an apologist argues in the words of Dr. Paley, the English theologian, that "there are falsehoods that are no lies . . . a criminal pleading not guilty; an advocate asserting the justice, or his belief in the justice, of his client's cause . . . no confidence is destroyed, because none is reposed; no promise to speak the truth is violated, because none is given."

I must confess to a dislike for this last piece of casuistry. I object to the reference to advocates immediately after criminals; and I do not relish the implications of the statement that the falsehoods of an advocate are not to be regarded as lies because nobody will believe them. But, whatever form of words may be used, the truth is that many people feel that the successful practice of law, particularly in criminal cases, is incompatible with conduct which is in the highest degree honorable, and with speech and thought which are in the highest degree candid. And the further truth is that this feeling is centered about the supposed duty of a lawyer in what are commonly referred to as "unjust causes."

The accepted legal canons defining that duty have been stated many times, but unfortunately for the most part in books which are to be found only in the hands of lawyers and students of law. My purpose is not so much to restate them as to set down my own observations about the problem of unjust causes. If what I have to say is almost entirely concerned with the defense of accused persons, the reason lies in the fact that criminal practice, as all the world knows, presents the question under consideration in its most acute and debatable form. Like most lawyers in active practice in small cities, I have tried both civil and criminal cases, often with an intimate knowledge of surrounding circumstances and an opportunity for insight into hidden motives that are not possible of attainment in our larger centers of population; but apart from this experience I cannot claim to speak with any special authority either as a lawyer or as a moralist. I am comforted, however, by the conviction that at all events I know as much about the practice of morality as Dr. Paley did about the practice of law.

There are four sources of information from which a lawyer representing a defendant in a criminal prosecution may be said with any degree of accuracy to "know that his client is guilty": (1) the entry of a plea of guilty in open court; (2) personal observation, as by having actually witnessed the commission of the offense; (3) a confession privately made by the client; and (4) such an "assemblage of probabilities," whether resulting from the weight of the evidence in favor of conviction or otherwise, as to amount to a moral certainty. This classification appears to me to be exhaustive. It is obvious that, in the first case supposed, no question of legal ethics is involved, since a defendant in pleading guilty instantly brings to an end the prosecution against him by his own solemn and deliberate act. It is likewise obvious that, in the second case supposed, the ethical question involved is a very simple one—no man ought to appear in the same proceeding both as a witness and as an advocate, and accordingly a lawyer should refuse professional employment in a cause in which he has such a knowledge of the facts at first hand as might require him to offer himself for examination on the witness stand.

The duty of a lawyer to whom a client has made a private confession of guilt is, under ordinary circumstances, equally simple—he ought to advise his client to plead guilty, and if the client refuses to do so he ought to withdraw from the case. In practice private confessions are much less common than is generally supposed. I can give but two instances from my own experience.

On the first occasion, I was retained by a Negro who had been indicted for larceny. I asked him what his defense was, and he replied that he was guilty, but that he guessed he "had better deny it in court," and that, if he did so, his "word would be as good as hers" (the prosecutrix's). I told him that in my opinion he ought to plead guilty, and after only a very little hesitation he did so with the utmost good humor.

On the second occasion, I was consulted by an intelligent white man who was being prosecuted for conducting a gambling house. He told me that the prosecution against him was a frame-up; he did run a gambling house, but the game was straight and his arrest was the act of players who had lost their money and who had proved to be poor losers. I asked him whether the general public frequented his house and whether he got a rake-off on the game, and he answered both questions in the affirmative. I then said to him that on his own statement it was manifest that he was violating the statute, and that I would not represent him unless he were willing to enter a plea of guilty. He went out of the office without making any special comment on what I had told him. Some weeks afterward it was brought to my attention that he had retained other counsel. Under the circumstances, I felt sufficiently interested in the case to make it my business to find out what happened at the trial. The defendant testified that friends of his sometimes came to his house to play poker and sometimes played for money, but that the public was not admitted; that the game was straight; and that he did not get a rake-off. The verdict of the jury was "not guilty." I do not think for a moment that the reputable and experienced advocate who tried the case for the defense acted improperly. I am satisfied, on the contrary, that the defendant learned some law during the course of his conference with me, and, having duly digested it, amended his story to meet the requirements of an acquittal.

A somewhat novel view, though one not fundamentally inconsistent with what has been said, was expressed by the Earl of Birkenhead, former Lord Chancellor of Great Britain, in an address delivered at a banquet of the American Bar Association, on August 31, 1923. "If," he said, "you take the extremest case of all, the case where it has been put at its strongest against the ethical situation of our profession, the case where a confession has been made by a prisoner to an advocate—I would meet that case without hesitation. It arose once at a critical stage of a great English litigation. I would meet that by saying, 'You are not to be the judge of whether that confession is made under an aberration, under a delusion, in hysteria; you are to put the whole facts of that case as those facts are known to you before the jury and before the judge, and they and not you are to decide as to the facts that have been proved, and as to the reliability of that which has been admitted.' " This amounts to saying to the defendant, "Do not plead guilty, because guilt and innocence are matters of law which you are incompetent to decide. Tell the whole truth in open court, and the judge and jury will draw the proper conclusion." I am disposed to think that I should adopt this procedure in a capital case, because false confessions of guilt, whether induced by mental abnormalities or an unselfish though perhaps misguided wish to shield the real offender, are not particularly uncommon. But in cases of minor importance, where the facts are comparatively simple and there is no reason to suspect hysteria or deliberate deception, it seems to me unnecessarily scrupulous to oppose the defendant's willingness to enter a formal plea of guilty.

The "great English litigation" to which Lord Birkenhead referred was doubtless that resulting from the death of Lord William Russell, an old man, who was found murdered in his bed in May 1840. His valet, Courvoisier, who was a Swiss citizen, was arrested and tried for the murder and was defended by Mr. Charles Philips, an eminent barrister of that day. The defendant denied his guilt, and the evidence against him was purely circumstantial. On the second day of the trial, which lasted three days, Courvoisier was identified in the yard of the prison by Mrs. Charlotte Pioalaine, the wife of a Frenchman who kept a hotel in a neighborhood of doubtful repute. According to her statement Courvoisier had placed in her hands for safe keeping a package which, on being opened, was found to contain silverware marked with the Russell coat of arms. Courvoisier saw her when she was inspecting the prisoners and immediately afterwards demanded an interview with his counsel. In the course of this interview he confessed that he had murdered his master, but insisted nevertheless that Philips should defend him to the uttermost.

What happened thereafter is unfortunately disputed, but I state the facts as Philips contended them to be. In great distress of mind Philips laid the situation before Baron Parke, who was sitting in the case with Chief Justice Tindal but who had taken no active part in the trial, and was advised that under the circumstances he was bound to go on with the case and to advance on his client's behalf every fair argument arising from the evidence. This Philips did. Under the rules of evidence then in force the defendant in a criminal prosecution was not permitted to testify. Accordingly Courvoisier was not called, and could not have been called, as a witness. In a closing speech which Baron Parke afterwards characterized as "perfectly unexceptionable," Philips pointed out the weaknesses and defects in the evidence produced by the Crown and exhorted consideration and pity by the jury for a stranger in a strange land who stood charged with so frightful a crime against one of their own people. The jury rendered a verdict of guilty and Courvoisier was duly executed.

It is apparent that the course which Baron Parke advised Philips to adopt cannot be reconciled with the one which Lord Birkenhead has said he would himself follow in a similar case.

Though the rules of evidence to which Philips was required to conform made it impossible for him to call Courvoisier as a witness, the real issue is one of ethics rather than of law and is not to be obscured by artificial rules. The underlying principle at least is clear enough—*in any case, whether civil or criminal, an advocate may properly do and say on his client's behalf whatever the client might properly do and say on his own behalf if he possessed the requisite legal training and skill.* It follows that a lawyer to whom an accused person has made a private confession of guilt may not permit the accused to testify to what he knows to be untrue. He may not offer evidence in support of an alibi or other affirmative defense which he knows to be untrue. He may not advance any argument (as Philips was charged with doing in the Courvoisier case) the effect of which might be to cast suspicion on an innocent person. So much may be taken for granted.

It has been argued,[1] however, that no legal or moral duty rests on a criminal to confess his guilt, and that in consequence his attorney may without impropriety object to the competency of the court or to the admissibility of evidence and may argue (as Philips admittedly did) that the evidence as a whole is insufficient to prove that the accused is guilty of the offense charged.

The reasoning in support of the premises on which this conclusion is founded may be summarized as follows. A criminal is under no legal duty to confess his crime, because no statutes exist either commanding confession or penalizing a failure to confess. On the other hand the moral duties of a criminal are those of every wrongdoer—to repent and (if possible) to make restitution. If a further duty of confession exists, it must be because the offender believes, or ought to believe, either that his punishment will benefit himself; or that it will deter others from committing like offenses; or, finally,

[1] E.g., by Harrison Hewitt, Esq., in the *Connecticut Bar Journal* for April 1927.

that he is so dangerous a person as to make it necessary that he be imprisoned or executed for the protection of society. The first two of these reasons may be shown to be unsound, and a proper evaluation of the last requires in any given case a detachment of view which a criminal can hardly be expected to possess.

Speculations such as these lead far into the realm of fine-spun casuistry. Let it suffice for present purposes that I cannot accept the general proposition that a criminal is under no moral duty to confess his crime. As it seems to me, the rule must be stated otherwise, though the existence of exceptions must instantly be admitted. If the death penalty were imposed (as it once actually was) for the theft of a loaf of bread, I should not advise a hungry man who had stolen a loaf of bread to plead guilty to an indictment charging him with the theft. If there were a state in the Union (the condition is happily contrary to fact) in which a statute made it a criminal offense for a father to teach the theory of evolution to his child, I should not advise a father who had taught his child what he believed to be true to submit himself to the penalties prescribed by the statute. A discussion of the reasons giving rise to real or apparent exceptions of this sort would involve an inquiry into the source of the sanctity of law—a subject which is touched upon in other chapters of this book and which has no place in the present connection.

Defenders of the conduct of Philips in the Courvoisier case have been accustomed to base their defense upon the extraordinary circumstances of a confession made to an advocate in the actual course of trial and to point out that if Philips had abandoned the case the legal rights of his client would have been seriously compromised. I am not impressed by this argument. Courvoisier had presented himself to Philips as an innocent man. Upon his statement to that effect Philips had advised him to enter a plea of not guilty and had consented to undertake his defense. Having undertaken it, Philips was in duty bound to express to the court and jury his client's contention respecting the matters charged against him. If Courvoisier's version of the facts changed during the course of the trial, he could not complain, as I see it, if his attorney's advice to him underwent a similar change. In my opinion Philips should have withdrawn from the case, unless Courvoisier had been willing either to plead guilty or to authorize Philips to present in some other way to the tribunal trying the case the substance of the statement which he had received from his client in private.

But though one accused of crime persist in a denial of the charge against him both in public and in private, the evidence of his guilt may be little short of overwhelming. Moreover, his statement of what occurred may be inherently improbable, and his reputation, both generally and in connection with the previous commission of offenses like the one concerned, may be equivocal or notorious. These considerations and a hundred others, slighter perhaps but none the less persuasive, may create a settled conviction in the mind of his attorney that the accused is indeed "guilty in manner and form as he stands indicted." Of course a lawyer is not in the position of an innkeeper and a common carrier—that is, bound to render service to whosoever claims it—and he is professionally free to withdraw from such a case. He is likewise professionally free to proceed with it.[2] But is he morally free to do so?

It is, I think, here rather than in the instance of a private confession that the current of public opinion sets "at its strongest against the ethical situation" of the legal profession. A lawyer who continues to defend a client from whose lips he

[2] "It is the right of the lawyer to undertake the defense of a person accused of crime, regardless of his personal opinion as to the guilt of the accused; otherwise innocent persons, victims only of suspicious circumstances, might be denied proper defense."—Canons of Ethics adopted by the American Bar Association.

has received a private confession of guilt is, after all, in most instances only a dishonest lawyer; but a lawyer who urges a defense which he believes to be false may be held, arguably enough, to be at the least a disingenuous man, and his disingenuousness may well appear the more significant and corroding because he is subjected to no sort of professional discipline or censure on account of it. The first judgment condemns only the particular advocate who has been false to his trust, but the second condemns all advocates and calls into question not only trial by jury but every system of administering justice of which advocacy is a part.

Whatever the system may be, the *dramatis personae* of all criminal prosecutions are the same, an accuser and an accused person, and the problems presented are those of determining what actually happened in respect to the matters with which the defendant stands charged and what the consequences to the defendant ought to be. Our ancestors experimented with a number of ways of solving these problems, such as trial by ordeal and by wager of battle, and finally adopted the expedient of submitting disputed matters of fact to the finding of twelve laymen and matters of law to the decision of a single judge. With the merits and defects of the jury system I am not at the moment concerned. Let it suffice, for present purposes, that it represents our method of answering the question, "What happened?" and that this question must be answered somehow whenever a criminal accusation is made on the one hand and denied on the other.

In the conduct of trial by jury, "the advocate," as Dr. Johnson said, "is not to usurp the functions of the judge; the advocate is to make himself the mouthpiece of him who is accused." He is likewise not to usurp the functions of the jury. To suggest that he ought to do so is in effect to propose that the jury system be replaced by some other method of finding facts.

When, therefore, the argument is advanced—as I heard it advanced not long ago by a professor in a theological seminary—that a lawyer ought not to defend a prisoner whom "all the decent people in the community know to be guilty," the criticism really intended is rather of due process of law as at present constituted in the United States than of the conduct of any particular lawyer or even of lawyers in general. Since the defendant in the case giving rise to the discussion had in fact been acquitted, the form of the criticism is perhaps to be attributed to righteous indignation at a real or supposed miscarriage of justice. Certainly the substitution of what "all the decent people in the community know" for the verdict of a jury which has at least listened to evidence and had an opportunity of seeing the parties face to face would seem to amount to a reversal of the classical precedent by appealing from Philip sober to Philip drunk. But in any event it is contrary to a common sense of fairness to try accused persons more than once for the same offense. If we are prepared to abolish trial by jury as the method by which legal guilt or innocence is to be determined, let us amend our laws accordingly. But until we do so, and until we make a law that a man shall be deemed guilty when his defense does not succeed in convincing his own lawyer, an advocate has no more justification for sitting in judgment on his client's cause than the members of a jury have for assuming the roles of partisans, or than a judge has for passing upon the credibility of witnesses.

But the assumption by a lawyer of a judicial attitude is not merely bad as a matter of logic. It is bad in practice as well, because a lawyer's opinion as to guilt or innocence is as fallible as that of anyone else. One of the first criminal cases in which I ever took part was a prosecution in which I was retained by the defendant, who had been indicted for stealing a dog. I asked him what his defense was and he told me that the dog had been given to him by a man whose name he had forgotten. Since the defendant had been in jail awaiting trial for about six weeks and presumably had had ample time to think matters over, this lapse of memory appeared to me exceedingly odd. Moreover, the defense on which he relied is humorously referred to by lawyers as the "mysterious stranger" defense, and there is a tradition that when it is interposed unsuccessfully, as it almost invariably is, the court is accustomed to add a few months to the usual sentence, on the theory that the defendant is not only guilty but gifted with very poor powers of invention besides. In brief, I did not believe a word of what my client told me. Being somewhat influenced by that fact as well as very inexperienced, I tried the case badly. For some reason which I have never been able to understand the defendant was acquitted. Perhaps the jury thought that, under the law, he was entitled to a better lawyer.

About six months afterward an accident put me in possession of the true facts of the case. The story told by my client was, as I had suspected, false, but he was nevertheless entirely innocent. The dog had been stolen by his sister's husband, and the defendant, who was unmarried, had come to the conclusion that with winter coming on it would be better for him to go to jail than to have his sister and her children deprived of the support and comfort to be expected from his erring brother-in-law.

Perhaps it may fairly be asked whether this incident is better suited to "point a moral or adorn a tale," and whether a proper answer would not confine it to the latter purpose. Certainly its hero, though he was innocent of being a thief, was an unabashed perjurer who remains, so far as I know, unrepentant to this very hour. And yet when, as happens from time to time, I see him working at his trade as a stonemason on some building in course of erection and he waves a greeting to me as I pass, I cannot help feeling grateful that the legal conviction of a defendant is not made to depend upon the conscientious conviction of his attorney.

That "the advocate is to make himself the mouthpiece" of his client is a figure of speech which is not entirely accurate. But taking the figure at its strongest we are still a long way from the conclusions of Dr. Paley. According to that authority, a lawyer may assert "his belief in the justice of his client's cause," and, though the assertion be a "falsehood," it is nevertheless "no lie." Any respectable lawyer can preach a simpler and sounder doctrine.[3] It is his duty to present to the court and jury his client's version of the facts, as well as every argument and inference which may fairly be drawn in the latter's favor. It is the duty of the jury to decide the case on the evidence as it comes from the mouths of the witnesses and the law as it comes from the mouth of the trial judge. If, therefore, an advocate makes by way of argument an honest statement of his opinion, he nevertheless acts improperly, since his opinion is either relevant—as it might be on the subject of previous good character—in which event he ought to have been sworn as a witness, or irrelevant, in which event he ought to be silent. If, on the other hand, his statement is dishonestly made, he is in no different position either personally or professionally from any other man who makes dishonest statements.

Perhaps no formal code of ethics can do more than to condemn the expression by an advocate of his personal beliefs about the character and conduct of his client. To stop here is nevertheless to leave something unsaid. Everyone who

[3] "It is improper for a lawyer to assert in argument his personal belief in his client's innocence or in the justice of his cause." Canons of Ethics adopted by the American Bar Association.

has sat for any considerable period of time in a courtroom has listened to the closing speech of at least one lawyer, who, like the player in Hamlet,

> Could force his soul so to his own conceit
> That from her working all his visage wann'd,
> Tears in his eyes, distraction in 's aspect,
> A broken voice, and his whole function suiting
> With forms to his conceit.

Whatever words may be used by such a pleader, it is obvious that he makes a representation as to the state of his emotions which is intended to incline the scales in his client's favor by the weight of his own influence. Jury speeches of this kind are, I believe, both less common and less generally effective than they were a half century ago—a result which is no doubt to be attributed as much to an improved taste as to a regenerated morality. The degree of conscious deception involved differs, of course, in individual cases, and no hard and fast rule can be laid down.

In this and in every like connection there is, however, one proposition from which no escape can be found. There is no room for an esoteric morality in the legal profession or in any other. Sir Edward Coke's classic definition of a burglar is "he that by night breaketh and entereth into a mansion house with intent to commit a felony." Accordingly, one indicted for burglary at common law was entitled to an acquittal upon showing that he broke into a mansion house by day instead of by night, or that he entered with the consent of the owner instead of by breaking, or that he broke into a shop instead of a mansion house, or that his original breaking was without intent to commit a felony.

It is beside the point to say that these are technical defenses. The answer is that they are no more technical than the crime itself, and that crime will always be to a greater or less degree a technical matter. But sin is not a technical matter. The conscience is a more sacred tribunal than any court. A righteous lawyer is first of all a righteous man. What is candid and honorable in private life retains those characteristics before a judge and jury, and no principle of ethics is sound which declares a liar to be a less despicable figure in a courtroom than anywhere else.

V

THE CASE FOR THE JURY

DOUBTLESS the way to administer justice most efficiently would be to abolish trial by jury and put a Solomon in every courtroom; just as the way to govern the world most efficiently would be to abolish democracy and put a Marcus Aurelius in every capital. The supply of supermen is, however, never equal to the demand for them; nor is the supply itself either constant or predictable. Every Solomon is as likely as not to be followed by a Rehoboam, and every Marcus Aurelius by a Commodus. These considerations suggest that in every discussion of the merits of the jury system the question involved is not so much whether trial by jury is good or bad in an absolute sense, as whether something reasonably more promising has been offered to replace it. Among the substitutes which have been suggested are trial by a single judge, by a court consisting of "three or more expert judges," [1] and by a tribunal composed of a judge, a junior member of the bar, and a "substantial business man." [2]

It may be noted in passing that while expertness is a quality which must always be regarded as desirable in judges, the reputation for wisdom enjoyed by the "substantial business man" has been somewhat impaired since the last of these suggestions was made. But indeed the practical answer to all such proposals is that if experience has shown that some juries are stupid, capricious, and corrupt, it has likewise shown that some judges (as well as some lawyers and business men) are stupid, capricious, and corrupt, too. Moreover, in the nature of things, no jury can render more than one bad verdict; whereas a bad judge may, and usually does, remain in authority for life or for a long term of years. A further answer

[1] Gregory Mason in *World's Work*, November 1928.
[2] Russell Duane in *The Forum*, October 1928.

is that some incorruptible judges are nevertheless—as juries never are—arrogant, unduly technical in their decisions, unfeeling and dilatory. No jurists in English history were more justly celebrated for learning than the Chancellors; but it was in the High Court of Chancery—where juries never sat—that men, seeing only ruined and disappointed suitors and undetermined causes, cried out bitterly for law and trial by jury, if what they saw was equity.

But we who are heirs to the political traditions of England and of those English rebels who became the first citizens of the United States, must, unless we reject our heritage, dismiss as inconclusive any argument against the jury system which is based on efficiency alone. We must dismiss any such argument because trial by jury is part and parcel of that sort of democracy which, as nearly all authorities agree, constitutes the special and peculiar contribution of the Anglo-Saxon race to the political wisdom of the world. Its underlying principle is that the sanctity of law arises not from the fiat of any potentate, however benevolent, nor from the vote of any majority, however enlightened, but from the common judgment and consent of the whole body of the people. This principle is reiterated in nearly all our great state papers, and in the practical application of it the jury system plays, and has always played, a vital and important part. In other words, no consideration of trial by jury can be adequate which ignores its political and legislative significance, and seeks to reduce it to the mere method of finding facts which the passion for logic of judges and lawyers has tried to make it.

When I came to the bar there was no class of cases in which juries were so much criticized as in suits for damages arising from industrial accidents. The courts had laid down a variety of rules as to the master's liability in such cases. They had held, of course, that the injured servant or employee could not recover it he had been guilty of contributory negligence. They had likewise held that, under certain circumstances, the servant had "assumed the risks" of his employment, and that even though no act or omission on his part had contributed to his injury he was not entitled to damages if his injury resulted from the negligence of a fellow servant. These determinations constituted what is sometimes called "judge-made law." (I am not using the words in a derogatory sense; here, as always, the important question is: "Is it good law?")

At all events, the juries, if they got a chance to decide the cases at all, invariably found in favor of the plaintiffs, no matter what the evidence was; and it was widely stated that the jury system had broken down in the determination of causes brought by injured employees against their employers, and that some change in the law would have to be made. The latter part of this conclusion, at least, was sound, though belated. The result was that the legislatures of a large majority of the States adopted Workmen's Compensation Laws providing for the care and partial reimbursement of injured employees, irrespective of the nature of the accidents in which they were injured. This is exactly the principle which juries had followed as best they could from the very beginning of the industrial age. Nor are Workmen's Compensation Laws in any objectionable sense class legislation, because they have proved quite as satisfactory to employers as to employees. I doubt, indeed, whether any respectable number of employers can be found who would return to the old system.[3]

A man may, if he pleases, dismiss this entire illustration by saying that it proves merely that juries in a given sort of case consistently violated their oaths for almost a hundred years. In the light of history this seems to me a foolish saying. Or

[3] I am indebted for this excellent illustration to "The Present-Day Jury System: a Defense," an article by Mr. Connor Hall which appeared in the *American Bar Association Journal* for February 1924.

he may say—as I think wisely—that in this particular connection it took our formal legislative machinery almost a hundred years to respond to the popular will, and that the fact that justice was done in the end is to be attributed very largely to the results of trial by jury.

For justice, in the sense in which the law seeks to enforce it and in the sense in which I am using the word, is not something conceived by *a priori* reasoning in the mind of a philosopher. Though it be true, as Spinoza said, that God is beyond our little good and evil, yet it is precisely with this human good and evil that the administration of justice is chiefly concerned. Still less is justice to be defined by the technical rules and refinements of judges and lawyers. Almost numberless legislative enactments—of which one of the earliest is the Statute of 12, Edward I, and one of the latest the Act of Congress of February 26, 1919—declare that in the decision of cases the courts shall not be bound by form or method, but shall give judgment according to the very right of the cause, and bear witness to the passionate insistence with which the men of our race have protested, generation after generation, against inherent professional formalism.

Justice is rather, for every man, the product of the changing definitions of his own race and age. It must assert social and economic convictions as they are, not as they might be. It must hold him who steals my purse to be a criminal, though posterity may perhaps conclude—as I think it will not—that communism is preferable to a system of private property. To speak wisely and well, it must speak humanly and in the present tense. In a word, common justice is the only justice worth having in this world, and the only way to make it better is by the slow process of breeding better men.

I once took part in a public debate on the subject of trial by jury. In the course of it my opponent quoted a saying of Wendell Phillips to the effect that the jury system "worked out a rough, average justice," and added that if each of two litigants had a just claim to $5,000, and a jury were to give $2,000 to one and $8,000 to the other, the kind of justice administered would be both "average" and "rough." No one will dissent from this conclusion; but the language used implies a determination of the very point which is in issue in every lawsuit: What constitutes *a just claim* to recover a judgment for money or some other relief against the defendant?

Suppose that a petty tradesman negligently injures, on successive days and in an identical manner, a millionaire and an unskilled laborer, and that both injured parties bring suits for damages. Shall the millionaire and the laborer be awarded like amounts because they have sustained like injuries? Shall the millionaire receive more than the laborer because his time is of greater value? Shall the laborer receive more than the millionaire because the loss of his time has inflicted upon him a relatively greater hardship? Finally, shall the financial situation of the defendant be considered in determining the several amounts which he must be called upon to pay? These are questions concerning which not all candid and intelligent men will agree, and on which a professional opinion is intrinsically no more representative or persuasive than any other. It is precisely the merit of trial by jury that it brings into our courtrooms, from day to day, the simple though deliberate views of those not technically trained as to what justice really is.

I should feel much less confidence in the results obtained if anything less than a unanimous verdict might be rendered. *The function of a jury is not to vote. Its function is to deliberate*—and thus to come to a general opinion in the way in which Quakers are said to arrive at "the sense of the meeting." In the course of the enforced deliberation which takes place in every jury room it is the well-grounded and conscientious opinion which usually prevails.

Not long ago I listened to the trial of a Negro for the theft of approximately twenty dollars in bills of small denominations. No money had been found on the defendant's person at the time of his arrest. In other respects the evidence against him, though entirely circumstantial, was strong. The verdict of the jury was not guilty. After the verdict had been rendered one of the jurors came to my office on business and in the course of our conversation discussed the case with me. On the first ballot the jurors had stood eleven to one for conviction. The single dissenter was a woman who had been born and brought up south of the Mason and Dixon line. During the discussion occasioned by the failure of the jury to agree on the first ballot she pointed out that although three or four days had elapsed between the commission of the crime and the defendant's arrest, and although the defendant's whereabouts and behavior during this period had been fully accounted for, there was no evidence that he had spent any money or that any money had been seen in his possession. On the basis of these facts she argued that he must be innocent. She assured the other jurors that she knew all about Negroes of the class to which the defendant belonged and that the theory of the case presented by the Commonwealth was psychologically impossible—if the defendant had been guilty he could not have resisted the temptation to spend the money at the first opportunity or at least to show it to his friends. The eleven jurors who had voted to convict were so much impressed by this argument that after a discussion lasting only about half an hour they voted unanimously to bring in a verdict of not guilty.

I have no opinion as to the guilt or innocence of the defendant who was acquitted or as to the validity of the reasoning on which his acquittal was founded, though my informant, a man of much more than ordinary intelligence, was satisfied in both particulars. The point with which I am concerned is that he and his fellows were convinced by an argument which not only had not occurred to any of them in the first place but *which would never have had a hearing if anything less than a unanimous verdict had been permitted.*

Even wilful misbehavior on the part of one or more jurors is not always sufficient to defeat the ends of justice. I have in mind a case which was recently tried in the courts of my own county, in which the evidence against the defendant, a public official, was so overwhelming that no verdict other than that of guilty appeared to be possible. The jury to which the case was submitted twice reported to the court that it had been unable to agree, and on each occasion was simply instructed to resume its deliberations. At the end of almost thirty hours the expected verdict of guilty was rendered. The moment the jury had been discharged it was plain to be seen what had gone on in the jury room—two of the jurors stood apart from their fellows and were visibly shaken men. If, as seems almost certain, they had corruptly held out in the defendant's interest, they had learned at first hand that the weight of righteous conviction is a phrase which amounts to more than a mere figure of speech. I am persuaded that for every case in which the requirement of a unanimous verdict results in a miscarriage of justice, there are a dozen cases in which a small minority of the jury—sometimes even a minority of one—induces the voluntary acceptance by the majority of a sound and sensible conclusion which, except for the requirement, would never have been fairly considered.

I might very well stop here and rest my defense of the jury system upon the propositions that trial by jury is an essential part of Anglo-Saxon democracy; that, in the complicated legislative process which democracy entails, "jury-made law" has on the whole proved more authentic and more truly representative of the popular will than "judge-made law;" and that for practical purposes common justice is preferable to justice of any other sort—even to that which might be held on theoretical grounds to be actually "more just." It is worth mentioning in this connection that the British in Afghanistan and elsewhere in the East have found it necessary to accept the last of these propositions and to enforce judicially merely the custom of the country, rather than to impose on Eastern peoples the alien, though perhaps higher, standards of the West.

Still, the charge is often made that jurors are generally incompetent, by reason of ignorance and prejudice, to decide the cases which are submitted to them; or, as I once heard the charge somewhat naïvely expressed, that the jury system compels the "business magnate" to accept judgment at the hands of "less than his peers." I am aware that statements of this sort cannot be established or refuted by mere assertions or denials, but I cannot leave the subject without recording my own opinion for whatever it may be worth.

"Is it likely," asks Mr. Jerome Frank in his recent book, *Law and the Modern Mind*, "that twelve men, summoned from all sorts of occupations, unaccustomed to the machinery of the law, unacquainted with their own mental workings and not known to one another, can, in the scant time allowed them for deliberation, do as good a job in weighing conflicting testimony as an experienced judge? Can they as well see through the story of the glib liar, or of the unconsciously biased but conscientious witness, or as ably allow for the stage fright which often makes the honest but cautious man speak falteringly on the witness stand?"

The reader will remember that the "three judges" who were presented to him at the beginning of this chapter were described as "expert." Mr. Frank's judge is "experienced" and his jury consists of "twelve men . . . unacquainted with their own mental workings." As a piece of pure dialectics I suppose the answer to Mr. Frank's questions must be that one man assumed to be competent is certain to do a better job in anything from laying bricks to weighing conflicting testimony than twelve men assumed to be incompetent—which is a truism or worse. However, not all judges are either expert or experienced and—since even psychologists are subject to call for jury duty—it can hardly be argued that all jurors are unacquainted with their own mental workings. Incidentally, where abuses in the selection of jurors exist, and corrupt politicians fill the jury wheel with the names of ward-heelers, it is entirely likely that the judges whom these same politicians place upon the bench are no better than they should be.

But my quarrel with Mr. Frank does not end with his experienced judge and his ignorant jurors. These characterizations are indeed not always or necessarily correct, but his reference to the scant time allowed to jurors for deliberation is never correct. The deliberations of a judge result solely from his own sense of humility and responsibility; the cocksure and opinionated judge rarely deliberates. On the other hand—and for reasons already shown—the deliberations of the jury room arise in the very nature of the case and require the evaluation and reconciliation of the conflicting points of view of the twelve jurors concerned.

Subject to the corrections noted, I am now ready to set down my answers to Mr. Frank's questions. In my opinion, twelve jurors usually do a much better job in weighing conflicting testimony than a judge. This is so partly because the jurors are "summoned from all sorts of occupations"—and therefore bring to their task a more diversified experience than is likely to be possessed by a single judge; partly because they are "unaccustomed to the machinery of the law"—and therefore listen to the testimony without technical preconceptions; partly because they are "not known to one another"—and therefore attach no special authority to one another's opinions; and very largely because of the automatic deliberation which trial by jury insures. Such men usually "see through the story of the glib liar or of the unconsciously biased but conscientious witness" much better than a judge, and in particular allow more sympathetically than a judge for the stage fright of the honest but cautious witness, because their own unfamiliarity with the routine of the courtroom subjects them, to some extent at least, to the same sense of embarrassment by which the witness is affected.

Finally, I am not impressed by the argument of the business magnate that the judgment which he receives from the average jury is the judgment of less than his peers. If most litigation turned on the statement and restatement of complicated accounts this argument—at least within some definitions of greater and less—might very well be sound. As a matter of fact, however, the question really at issue in the great majority of cases is not one of mathematics but of human veracity—a question which is at once one of the simplest and one of the most complicated under the sun. In the solution of it—and in the solution of every question involving the fundamentals of life, liberty, and property—I do not believe that the average business or professional man is wiser than the average farmer or carpenter. He is better educated in the formal sense and superficially more polished. He has a somewhat wider knowledge of current events and a more nearly adequate understanding of financial matters. On the other hand he has spent fewer hours alone, and accordingly has thought less for himself and is more easily influenced by stereotypes and catchwords. He is less simple and natural and his prejudices are at least as deeply rooted. These are general observations of the widest sort, and are, of course, without value unless clearly understood to be such. As among themselves, business magnates may, if they please, submit their differences to trial by a single judge or to arbitration by psychologists. I can only say that in a matter of the last moment to myself I had rather submit the issue to an "impartial jury of the vicinage."

VI
THE SANCTITY OF LAW

A GREAT Chief Justice of Massachusetts once said, "Obedience to law is liberty," and intended thereby, as I understand his words, to express the nature of liberty in terms of law. At the present time, much is being spoken and written in the United States about the menace of a growing disrespect for the sanctity of law, and much is likewise being spoken and written about the menace of a growing disrespect for the sanctity of liberty. If, therefore, there is such a connection between liberty and law as to warrant the definition of one in terms of the other, we ought to ask ourselves what this connection is. Or, to put the question less generally, if liberty is indeed obedience to law, we ought to ask ourselves what law is and whence comes that sanctity which it is said to possess.

The concept of law is, I suppose, one of the very oldest in the history of civilization. In every moderately advanced state of society except that of early England the word "law" has had only one significance—namely, a rule prescribed by a superior. A given situation has arisen and people have said, "What was the decree of the chief in cases like this?" or "What is the decree of the chief in this case?" or "Let the tribe vote to decide what shall be done," or "What do the wise men say?" or, what is in practice the same as the last, "What is the will of the god?" Now our Anglo-Saxon ancestors, at least in England, never asked questions or made statements at all like these. Instead they asked a paradoxical question. Whether the paradox implied in the question is true or false or partly true and partly false will appear hereafter. But the question was: "What is the law?" This means that our ancestors regarded the law, not as a rule laid down by anybody to meet the exigencies of a particular case or set of cases, but as an existing thing and a thing which had existed from "time whereof the memory of man runneth not to the contrary." To borrow a theological expression, they habitually thought of law as something begotten, not made.

One of the necessary results of this conception is interest in and regard for ancient customs. If the law is indeed immemorially old, there is no better evidence of what the law is than time-honored practices, and the older a practice is the better evidence it becomes. You remember what Sir Richard, the Norman, says about his Saxon friend in *Puck of Pook's Hill:*

> His Saxons would laugh and jest with Hugh, and Hugh with them, and—this was marvelous to me—if even the meanest of them said that such and such a thing was the Custom of the Manor, then straightway would Hugh and such old men of the Manor as might be near forsake everything else to debate the matter—I have seen them stop the mill with the corn half ground—and if the custom or usage were proven to be as it was said, why, that was the end of it, even though it were flat against Hugh, his wish and command. Wonderful!

So it came about in England that all men knew the exact rights of a widow in her deceased husband's estate and the precise penalty for cutting off a man's hand, not only centuries before there was a written law governing these subjects, but centuries before there was any formal declaration, whether written or oral, that a widow had any rights in her deceased husband's estate, or any formal prohibition against doing hurt to one's neighbor. And in theory, as I have said, a man did one thing and avoided another, not out of deference to custom, but out of deference to law. The law already existed and the custom was evidence of it—that was all.

A second paradox ought to be mentioned. In early English legislation the words "custom" and "liberty" were used almost interchangeably. Thus in chapter 13 of Magna Carta the "*liberties and customs*" of London and other cities and seaports were confirmed, and in chapter 39 of one of the first republications of the Charter it was provided that no freeman should be "disseised of his freehold or his *liberties or his free customs* or be outlawed or exiled or otherwise destroyed but by lawful judgment of his peers, or by the law of the land."

All this is interesting enough as a mere matter of legal history, but the really important questions are how much truth there is in the proposition that the law exists antecedently to any oral or written statement of it and in the seemingly disconnected proposition that, for some purposes at least, a custom is the same thing as a liberty.

In one sense—though a sense which is, I think, both narrow and superficial—the first proposition is certainly not true. I mean that when a new condition arises in the world—as, for instance, by the invention of the aeroplane—it is too much to suppose that there already exists a "rule of the sky," like the time-honored "rule of the road," to meet the precise condition thus created. All that the common law has to say about aeroplanes is that the owner of land owns the air above the land as high as to the sky—a pronouncement which was born in an age when a man could not make use of air to a greater height than he could build, and which consequently will not square with the facts of the present day.

But in a much wider and deeper sense, common law—if I may use that phrase somewhat loosely to refer to that sort of law which is practised before it is promulgated—is one of the most real and practical things under the sun—as real and practical as that common sense of which it is the legislative product—and all the major sanctions of our penal code are founded upon it.

Most people, for example, do not kill their neighbors or burn their neighbors' houses or steal their neighbors' goods, and in consequence we are all agreed that murder, arson, and robbery ought to be punished as crimes. Almost no one disputes these conclusions, least of all the very small percentage of persons who do in fact commit murder or arson or robbery. Even in the midst of the vile sort of sentimentality which sometimes surrounds a sensational murder trial, no special pleader is heard to argue, even by implication, that murderers ought to go unpunished. He only argues that for some reason or other his client is not really to be regarded as a murderer at all. In effect, this argument means that most persons in like situation with the defendant would have done exactly what he did. In the usual case the argument is a bad one because it is not true—most persons in like situation with the defendant would not have done what he did. The technical objection to defenses based upon the so-called "unwritten law" is that it is not written, but in the majority of cases the real objection is that it is not law.

What is even more important than the fact that most people do not commit crimes is the further fact that most people do not wish to commit them. The deepest of all the differences between the average good citizen and the average criminal is not a difference in will-power or self-control, but rather in the line of conduct which each is instinctively moved to follow. Where there is little will to obey there is little obedience among either good citizens or criminals. Anyone doubting this may, I think, profitably ask himself how many laws he has actually been tempted to break and what the result of his temptation was.

Until the present year there was a statute in my own state which forbade the operation of an automobile, under any circumstances, at a rate of speed greater than forty miles per hour. This statute set up a purely *a priori* standard of safety, which was at variance with that determined by current practice and judgment. The consequence was that most owners of automobiles, who had habitually driven at speeds in excess of forty miles per hour and believed that they had done so with entire safety to themselves and others, paid no attention to the statute. On the other hand, the great prohibitions of the penal code are founded upon a consensus of opinion and conduct just short of unanimity. If a man steals my purse he is said to be a robber—that is to say, a criminal. But if he sees no reason why he should not steal it he is said to be a kleptomaniac—that is to say, a madman.

But the effective obligation of customary law is not limited to those subjects on which its terms have been incorporated and expressed in some formal statute or decree. No such statute, for example, enjoins the payment of what are sometimes called "debts of honor"—or, less euphemistically, gambling debts. Indeed, the whole of our legislative and judicial logic is against their collection. If I seek to recover a thousand dollars on a note, the statutes will place at my disposal the courts with their writs and the sheriff with his bailiffs. I can seize and sell my debtor's tangible property and I can attach debts due him by others, including, in some states, his wages and earnings. As a last resort, I can go into the courts of the United States and procure the appointment of a trustee in bankruptcy to take charge of his estate. But if I seek to recover a thousand dollars on a bet the statutes will not help me at all. And yet, year in and year out, the most carefully managed corporation, which investigates and reinvestigates every customer to whom it extends credit, cannot, with all the machinery of the courts within its reach, collect so large a proportion of its debts as any gambler can collect without lifting a finger.

I am not arguing for or against the morality of gambling or of paying gambling debts, any more than I was arguing, a moment ago, as to the wisdom or safety of driving automobiles at any particular speed. I am only concluding the last of three observations of fact, which may be restated as follows. In the first place, when the requirements of a statute are the same as those of common opinion, as in the case of high crimes and misdemeanors, the statute is almost universally obeyed. In the second place, when the requirements of a statute are greater than those of common opinion, as in the case of the operation of automobiles, the statute is disobeyed by nearly all those who are without the will to obey it. In the third place, when the requirements of a statute are less than those of common opinion, as in the case of gambling debts, the latter is, nevertheless, almost universally obeyed, and it would seem —perhaps perversely—a little the more willingly because all the implications of the statute are the other way.

With these observations in mind we may now inquire what significance is to be found in the statement that a custom is a liberty. In pursuing this inquiry, something must be said, if only by way of definition, about the nature of democracy.

The word "democracy" is commonly used to mean, first, a political party—in the United States—as opposed to Republicanism; secondly, a form of government—sometimes called a pure democracy—as opposed to a republic; and, thirdly, a form of state, as opposed to a monarchy or an aristocracy. In what follows I am using the word only in the third sense.

Now democracy in this sense is indeed partly conceptual and approximate—becoming rather than being, evolving rather than evolved. The ideal democracy, like the kingdom of God, does not exist, and perhaps will never exist, on earth; but a faith in democracy presupposes, and the practice of democracy requires, the existence of a popular will which may be determined at least with a working degree of accuracy from day to day. Let me illustrate what I mean by referring to the common experience known as "making up one's mind" —a phrase which, rightly considered, is itself enlightening.

I suppose a man approaches most of the important questions of his life with conflicting preferences. Ambition urges him, let us say, to run for public office. Prudence suggests that in doing so he will be likely to neglect his business. Perhaps what he conceives to be his duty to his family impels him in one direction and what he conceives to be his duty to his state or nation in another. A dozen other considerations pull him this way and that. Some of these considerations may be selfish and some unselfish, or they may be all selfish or all unselfish. At any rate, after a longer or shorter period of indecision, the man is said to "make up his mind," and thereafter the whole man is determined to run for office or not to run, as the case may be. Democracy has staked everything upon the proposition that the mind of a people may be made up in like manner from the discordant inclinations of all the individuals concerned.

I am aware that the proposition just stated has been regarded as fanciful by certain modern writers who contend that democracy means the rule of the majority and nothing more. I do not wonder that these writers have little zeal for democratic institutions. If the United States were governed by a single despot who ordered my execution without trial, I should feel, to put it mildly, exceedingly ill used. But if the United States were governed by an oligarchy of one hundred and this oligarchy ordered my execution without trial, I should feel equally ill used. Finally, if the Constitution of the United States were amended in a perfectly lawful way—as it might be—so as to permit the President to prepare a list of persons to be executed, and the President, in the exercise of the discretion vested in him, selected me as one of his victims, I should not be comforted in the smallest degree by the assurance that a substantial majority of my fellow citizens were in favor of the whole proceeding. If this be democracy, there is indeed only one reason for being a democrat, and that a very selfish one—namely, that, whereas I should have only one chance in a hundred million of being the absolute monarch of the United

States and only one chance in a million of belonging to an oligarchy of a hundred, I have, as between myself and the whole number of voting electors, a little more than one chance in two of being on the winning side at every election. In brief, such a theory leaves the individual citizen, if he happens to be in the minority, as completely forgotten in a democracy as anywhere else.

But democracy, as I see it, is not fundamentally concerned with majorities or minorities at all. What democracy assumes is unanimity—that is to say, a common mind. This assumption is, in practice, never entirely true, and yet, as George Santayana has pointed out in a passage which I shall have occasion to quote at length in discussing the Fourteenth Amendment, we vote only about minor matters. The really significant fact about a presidential election in the United States is not how many voters are Democrats and how many Republicans, but rather that all of the voters presumably regard either a Democratic or a Republican administration as desirable from one point of view and at least tolerable from any other.

> Were this not the case, a decision by vote would be as alien a fatality to any minority as the decree of a foreign tyrant, and at every election the right of rebellion would come into play. . . . To leave a decision to the majority is like leaving it to chance—a fatal procedure unless one is willing to have it either way. . . . It is therefore actually required that juries, whose decisions may really be of moment, should be unanimous; and parliaments and elections are never more satisfactory than when a wave of national feeling runs through them and there is no longer any minority nor any need of voting.

Democracy, says Santayana, in substance, presupposes fundamental unanimity, and in a hearty and sound democracy the office of a representative assembly is only to announce the decision which has already been arrived at. The common law presupposes that laws are first born and afterward declared by judges and legislators. It is clear that these two suppositions are really one and the same; or, to put the matter in another way, that the Anglo-Saxon conception of law is essentially democratic in character.

The story of Robinson Crusoe may be regarded for political purposes as a parable in two parts. The first part is concerned with Crusoe alone upon his island. The poet has made him say that he was monarch of all he surveyed and that his right there was none to dispute; but his monarchy consisted of an uninhabited wilderness, and if there was none to dispute his right there was likewise none to assert it or to whom it might be asserted. Such a right is in effect no right at all.

In the second part of the story, Crusoe and Friday lived together on the island. The coming of Friday converted a solitude into a sovereign State, and Crusoe, like Louis XIV, was the State. Instead of shooting Friday, as he might have done, Crusoe told him that he might keep his life so long as he behaved himself in a specified way. What happened was not the proposal of a contract, but the publication of a constitution. The assent of Friday did not matter in the least. Because Crusoe had a gun, he had absolute power—that is to say, sovereignty—and a constitution is the declaration of a self-limited sovereignty. If Crusoe had afterward revoked the constitution and had shot Friday, the result would have been a sin but not a crime. On the other hand, if Friday had attempted to kill Crusoe, the result would have been treason if he had failed and revolution if he had succeeded. A revolution is either an actual shifting of sovereignty or a practical demonstration that the power theretofore believed to be sovereign is not really so.

Now the situation of Crusoe and Friday is, in miniature, that which has always existed and must always exist in every sovereign State, and it suggests the answer of the political philosopher to the question as to what law is. Law is the voice of sovereignty, and the essence of sovereignty is power. In the field of politics there are no "unalienable rights," because in the last analysis the power which grants a right can necessarily take it away. I do not think for a moment that the framers of the Declaration of Independence meant to assert the contrary. To suppose that they did so is to misread the very words of the declaration which they signed. When men take up arms, protesting that they do so to defend rights with which they have been "endowed by their Creator," they are not talking politics. Such men stand exactly where Friday would have stood if he had attacked Crusoe with a club—exactly where history shows that the framers of the Declaration of Independence actually did stand—that is, on the brink of revolution. Revolutions may be spoken of as political phenomena only in the way in which miracles may be spoken of as natural phenomena. They are outside of politics, just as miracles are outside of nature, and they are to be justified or condemned in the light of history and on moral rather than political grounds.

Nor is the essential quality of sovereignty different in a democracy from what it is in any other form of State. We are accustomed to speak of a system of checks and balances as one of the characteristics of our American form of democracy. The powers of Congress are limited by those of the President, and the powers of both Congress and the President are defined by the Supreme Court. In addition, various rights and immunities are expressly guaranteed, in whole or in part, by the Constitution of the United States. But a system of checks and balances and a bill of rights are no more than effective limitations upon the organs of government. Since the days of the Medes and the Persians, no people has been so foolish as to suppose that there can be, in logic or in fact, a law or a constitution which cannot be amended. If a constitutional provision set up the Supreme Court, a constitutional provision can strike it down; and if Congress is prohibited by the Constitution from making any law respecting an establishment of religion, the authority which declared that prohibition yesterday can revoke it tomorrow. There is somewhere in every sovereign State absolute, unlimited, and illimitable power, and from the decrees of this power the citizen of a democracy, as well as the subject of a monarchy or aristocracy, has, of necessity, no lawful protection and can take no lawful appeal.

And yet there is, as all men are aware, some vital and tremendous difference—reflected and expressed in a sort of fundamental optimism, whether well or ill founded—which distinguishes a democracy from a monarchy or an aristocracy more widely than either of these political forms is to be distinguished from the other. This difference is not to be found in the quality of sovereignty in a democracy, but rather in the source of it. For if, in a monarchy or an aristocracy, one man or a few men have sovereign power and the people are subject to them, in a democracy sovereign and subjects are, by definition, the same. The people are conceived as making those very laws which they are bound to obey.

"The common law," said Mr. Justice Holmes, "is not a brooding omnipresence in the sky but the articulate voice of some sovereign . . . that can be identified." In the act of identification we come face to face with the meaning of the saying that a custom is a liberty. There is no intrinsic sanctity in the decree of a monarch or the vote of a majority. In either case, the law laid down is merely good or bad according to the facts. But a law declaring the usage of a people is a holy law, because it finds its authority and verification in the hearts of those who are called upon to obey it. *When men obey such a law they are free men, because they command themselves.*

VII
THE TWO FOURTEENTH AMENDMENTS

THE Fourteenth Amendment to the Constitution of the United States was proposed by Congress to the legislatures of the several states on June 16, 1866, and was declared ratified by proclamation of the Secretary of State a little more than two years afterwards. The first section—which is the only living part of the amendment and which is sometimes referred to in what follows as if it were the whole—reads as follows:

> All persons born or naturalized in the United States, and subject to the jurisdiction thereof, are citizens of the United States and of the State wherein they reside. No State shall make or enforce any law which shall abridge the privileges or immunities of citizens of the United States; nor shall any State deprive any person of life, liberty, or property, without due process of law; nor deny to any person within its jurisdiction the equal protection of the laws.

As a matter of political theory, this language is that of the people of the United States. I propose, in the first place, to attempt to determine its intended meaning by an examination of the principal arguments advanced both for and against the adoption of the amendment in the debates in Congress, in the debates in the legislatures of the several states, and in discussions before the people at large. I call this intended meaning the first Fourteenth Amendment. The text of the Amendment has been many times considered and construed in decisions of the Supreme Court of the United States. I propose, in the second place, to refer to some of these decisions in order to discover the actual meaning of the language used as determined from day to day by our constitutional court of last resort. I call this actual meaning the second Fourteenth Amendment. Finally, I shall attempt to evaluate the political significance of the discrepancies which appear between the Constitution by electoral intention on the one hand and by judicial interpretation on the other.

1

The purpose of the Fourteenth Amendment was plainly remedial. The Civil War had come to an end. Slavery had been abolished by the Thirteenth Amendment. Nevertheless, Negroes remained subject to various disabilities in all the states south of the Mason and Dixon line and in many of those north of it. The Civil Rights Bill, directed by its express terms against discrimination among the inhabitants of any State or Territory on account of race or previous condition of slavery, had been passed over President Johnson's veto, but was generally believed to be unconstitutional. On these accounts the supporters of the Fourteenth Amendment were content in most instances to rest their case on a mere recital of the familiar sequence of the old law, the mischief and the remedy.

On May 8, 1866, Thaddeus Stevens, speaking in the House of Representatives, said:

> The first section [of the amendment] prohibits the States from abridging the privileges and immunities of citizens of the United States, or unlawfully depriving them of life, liberty, or property, or of denying to any person within their jurisdiction the "equal" protection of the laws.
>
> I can hardly believe that any person can be found who will not admit that every one of these provisions is just. They are all asserted, in some form or other, in our DECLARATION or organic law. But the Constitution limits only the action of Congress, and is not a limitation on the States. This amendment supplies that defect, and allows Congress to correct the unjust legislation of the States, so far that the law which operates upon one man shall operate *equally* upon all. Whatever law punishes a white man for a crime shall punish the black man precisely in the same way and to the

same degree. Whatever law protects the white man shall afford "equal" protection to the black man. Whatever means of redress is afforded to one shall be afforded to all. . . . Now different degrees of punishment are inflicted . . . according to the color of the skin. . . . I need not enumerate these partial and oppressive laws. Unless the Constitution should restrain them those States will all, I fear, keep up this discrimination, and crush to death the hated freedmen. Some answer, "Your civil rights bill secures the same things." That is partly true, but a law is repealable by a majority. And I need hardly say that the first time that the South with their copperhead allies obtain the command of Congress it will be repealed. . . .

Fifteen days later Senator Jacob M. Howard of Michigan presented to the Senate the joint resolution proposing the adoption of the amendment. Senator Howard had served as a member of the Reconstruction Committee by which the text of the amendment had been drafted, and therefore spoke with at least apparent authority. In the course of his remarks he pointed out that the citizens of each of the states had long enjoyed "a mass of privileges, immunities, and rights, some of them secured by the second section of the fourth article of the Constitution . . . some by the first eight amendments of the Constitution"; but that these privileges, immunities, and rights were protected only from legislation by Congress and not from legislation by the several states. The Senator continued:

The great object of the first section of this amendment is, therefore, to restrain the power of the States and compel them at all times to respect these great fundamental guarantees. . . . The last two clauses of the first section . . . disable a State from depriving not merely a citizen of the United States, but any person, whoever they may be, of life, liberty, or property without due process of law, or from denying to him the equal protection of the laws of the State. This abolishes all class legislation in the States and does away with the injustice of subjecting one caste of persons to a code not applicable to another. It prohibits the hanging of a black man for a crime for which the white man is not to be hanged. It protects the black man in his fundamental rights as a citizen with the same shield which it throws over the white man. . . . If adopted [the amendment will] . . . forever disable [the States] from passing laws trenching upon those fundamental rights and privileges which pertain to citizens of the United States, and to all persons who may happen to be within their jurisdiction. It establishes equality before the law, and it gives to the humblest, the poorest, and most despised of the race the same rights and the same protection before the law as it gives to the most powerful, the most wealthy, or the most haughty. . . .

The statements of Mr. Stevens and Senator Howard unquestionably represented the official attitude of the Republican majority in Congress, and were substantially repeated by other Republicans in the debates on the amendment which took place in the House and Senate. They were likewise substantially repeated in addresses to other deliberative bodies and in discussions directed to the general public.

Governor Andrew G. Curtin of Pennsylvania, in his message to the State Legislature which afterwards ratified the amendment, said:

I present, for your consideration, the amendments to the Constitution of the United States, proposed . . . by . . . Congress. . . . The amendments are so moderate and reasonable in their character, that it would [be] astonishing, if the people [should fail] to approve them. That every person, born in the United States, and free, whether by birth or manumission, is a citizen of the United States, and that no State has a right to abridge the privileges of citizens of the United States—these are principles which were never seriously doubted anywhere, until after the insane crusade in favor of slavery had been for some time in progress. What is called the decision of the Supreme Court of the United States, in the Dred Scott case, has made it expedient and proper to re-assert these vital principles in an authoritative manner, and this is done in the first clause of the proposed amendments. . . .

At that time Pennsylvania was the only state which reported in full the debates in its legislature. Senator Connell, speaking in favor of the amendment, quoted the law of Mississippi for the year 1865 making it a crime, punishable by a fine of not less than fifty dollars nor more than five hundred dollars, for the employee of any railroad to allow any freedman, Negro, or mulatto, except nurses with their mistresses, to ride in first-class passenger cars set apart for and used by white persons. After citing this statute, Mr. Connell declared that the adoption of the amendment was a political necessity on account of the state of things in the South. He added: "Not much Shakespeare about that. That section [of the statute quoted] gives one a glimpse of the poetry, refinement and humanity of Mississippi life."

Similar arguments—which perhaps appear to have been more temperately worded only because they were incompletely reported—were presented to the legislatures of Ohio, Illinois, Missouri, Indiana, Minnesota, Massachusetts, and various other states.

The issue raised by the proposal of the amendment was, of course, widely discussed in the press.

Carl Schurz, writing in the *Atlantic Monthly* for March 1867, declared that the first section was "intended to engraft the main provisions of the Civil Rights Act upon the Constitution," and this formed "a necessary complement of the abolition of slavery." To the same effect were editorial comments in the *New York Times*, *Harper's Weekly*, and other newspapers and periodicals. The *Times* particularly commended Senator Howard's opening statement in the Senate as "frank and satisfactory," and his exposition of the conditions leading up to the proposal of the amendment as "clear and cogent."

For present purposes, the grounds on which the amendment was opposed are of less importance than those on which it was supported. It is worth mentioning, however, that its opponents generally accepted without question the definition of the issue propounded by their adversaries. Samuel J. Randall, a Democrat from Pennsylvania, replying in the House to the arguments of Mr. Stevens and his followers, declared that the first section proposed to make an equality in every respect between the white and black races, notwithstanding the policy of discrimination which had theretofore been exclusively exercised by the states. In the opinion of this speaker there was "no occasion whatever for the Federal power to be exercised between the two races at variance with the wishes of the people of the States." In the same debate, Andrew J. Rogers, of New Jersey, a Democratic member of the House, called attention to the fact that the first section was admittedly neither "more or less than an attempt to embody in the Constitution . . . [the] outrageous and miserable civil rights bill," and asserted that since a Negro who was refused the right to be a juror would be deprived of his privileges and immunities as a citizen of the United States, the result of the amendment would be a revolution worse than the one through which the country had passed. Mr. Wallace, an opponent of the amendment in the legislature of Pennsylvania, said that the first and fifth sections taken together declared who were citizens and conferred upon Congress power to protect that citizenship. He defined privilege as "everything that . . . is desirable," and immunity as "a privileged freedom from anything painful," and contended that under the power conferred upon Congress by the second clause of section one, "the dearest rights" could be bestowed upon Negroes. The *Memphis Avalanche* said that the amendment had been the "war cry of the partisan leaders in the late struggle on the hustings and at the ballot-box," and that it meant to the Northern people Negro equality, social and political, not, however, applicable to themselves. The *Montgomery Mail* said that the chief objection to the amendment was the first section, which prohibited a state "from depriving [a Negro] of any rights or privileges which a white man [might] possess." The *New Orleans Picayune* characterized the first section as an incorporation into the Constitution of the Civil Rights Bill. Another opponent of the amendment asserted that it secured for the Negro the right to vote, to sit on juries, to enter hotels, lecture rooms, and so forth. A press correspondent, seemingly a Republican, said that the Democrats of Kentucky feared that Congress would be empowered by the amendment to confer the suffrage on Negroes; that it admitted Negroes to the witness stand, the jury box, street cars, good seats in public conveyances, good accommodations at hotels, the public schools, and all other civil rights which white people enjoyed; and that if it went this far, the Democrats reasoned that it might go farther.

In the nature of the case the foregoing summary is by no means exhaustive. *It is, however, sufficiently exhaustive to justify the statements that the purpose of the framers of the Fourteenth Amendment was to complete the work of emancipation by writing into the Constitution the provisions of the Civil Rights Bill, and that a large majority of its supporters and opponents believed that its principal, if not its only, effect would be to confer additional rights and immunities on members of the Negro race.*

At least one (and presumably a majority) of the members of the Supreme Court were originally of the same opinion. The amendment was first considered by the Court in the *Slaughter House Cases* decided in 1873. Mr. Justice Miller, who delivered the opinion of the Court, said:

> The institution of African slavery, as it existed in about half of the States of the Union, and the contests pervading the public mind for many years, between those who desired its curtailment and ultimate extinction and those who desired additional safeguards for its security and perpetuation, culminated in the effort, on the part of most of the States in which slavery existed, to separate from the

Federal Government, and to resist its authority. This constituted the war of the rebellion, and whatever auxiliary causes may have contributed to bring about this war, undoubtedly the overshadowing and efficient cause was African slavery.

The learned Justice then reviewed at some length the events leading up to the adoption of the Thirteenth, Fourteenth, and Fifteenth Amendments, and proceeded as follows:

We repeat, then, in the light of this recapitulation of events, almost too recent to be called history, but which are familiar to us all; and on the most casual examination of the language of these amendments, no one can fail to be impressed with the one pervading purpose found in them all, lying at the foundation of each, and without which none of them would have been even suggested; we mean freedom of the slave race, the security and firm establishment of that freedom, and the protection of the newly made freeman and citizen from the oppressions of those who had formerly exercised unlimited dominion over him. It is true that only the fifteenth amendment, in terms, mentions the Negro by speaking of his color and his slavery. But it is just as true that each of the other articles was addressed to the grievances of that race, and designed to remedy them as the fifteenth.

We do not say that no one else but the Negro can share in this protection. Both the language and spirit of these articles are to have their fair and just weight in any question of construction. . . . But what we do say; and what we wish to be understood is, that in any fair and just construction of any section or phrase of these amendments, it is necessary to look to the purpose which we have said was the pervading spirit of them all, the evil which they were designed to remedy, and the process of continued addition to the Constitution, until that purpose was supposed to be accomplished, as far as constitutional law can accomplish it.

These remarks were followed by a discussion of the several clauses composing the first section of the amendment. As to the concluding clause—"nor shall any State . . . deny to any person within its jurisdiction the equal protection of the laws"—the learned Justice observed:

> The existence of laws in the States where the newly emancipated Negroes resided, which discriminated with gross injustice and hardship against them as a class, was the evil to be remedied by this clause, and by it such laws are forbidden.
>
> . . . *We doubt very much whether any action of a State not directed by way of discrimination against the Negroes as a class, or on account of their race, will ever be held to come within the purview of this provision. It is so clearly a provision for that race and that emergency, that a strong case would be necessary for its application to any other.* (Italics added.)

In the entire field of judicial dicta it would be hard to find a prophecy which has been more completely discredited by the event.

2

Since the determination of the *Slaughter House Cases* the amendment has been interpreted by the Supreme Court in more than a thousand decisions. Many of these decisions have been concerned with the inevitable work of definition.

Thus a child born in the United States of Chinese parents becomes a citizen of the United States at the moment of his birth by virtue of the first clause of the amendment; but an unemancipated Indian, though born in the United States, is not subject to the jurisdiction thereof, and on this account is not a citizen within the meaning of the clause in question. A corporation is not a citizen and consequently does not enjoy those privileges and immunities which are secured to citizens against legislation by the states, but is a person and as such is protected against deprivation of property without due process of law and against a denial of the equal protection of the laws.

The prohibitions of the amendment are directed exclusively against action by the states and not against the misconduct of individuals. Since, however, a state can act in no other way than by its legislative, executive, or judicial agencies, the amendment is directed against the power of a state by whatever organ it may act, and applies not only to a state constitution or statute, but also to municipal ordinances or regulations adopted by state authority, and to wrongful action by a state court or by the officers of a state in administering a valid statute, though not to the unauthorized (and therefore merely advisory) instructions of a state officer such as a superintendent of weights and measures.

Contrary to the "great object" of the amendment as understood by Senator Howard, the privileges and immunities which are thereby protected are not the "great fundamental guarantees" enumerated in the Bill of Rights, but only those that belong to citizens of the United States as distinguished from citizens of the states, or those that arise from the Constitution and laws of the United States as contrasted with those that spring from other sources. It follows that while a state may not abridge the right of a citizen of the United States to pass from one state to another, or to protection on the high seas and in foreign countries, it may, if it sees fit, abridge his right to trial by jury in a state court.

Trial by jury is not only not a privilege of national citizenship, but is not a requisite of due process of law. Deprivation of due process, though not defined in the Constitution, may result from the taking of the property of a railroad company for private use under the asserted authority of a state board of transportation, from the attempted imposition on a utility company of confiscatory rates, and from the attempt by a state to subject to taxation property and rights not subject to its jurisdiction. A litigant has been denied due process of law where his case has been decided by a state supreme court in such a way that he has not had a proper opportunity to present his evidence, but not where a state court has erroneously admitted evidence or entered an erroneous decree after a full hearing. Freedom of contract and freedom of speech and of the press, though not included in the privileges and immunities of citizens of the United States, are nevertheless—the first under earlier and the second under later decisions—among the liberties protected by the due process clause.

All these liberties are, however, subject to regulation by the police power of the states. A state statute which restricts freedom of contract by fixing maximum hours of labor for both men and women constitutes a valid exercise of the police power, but until quite recently a similar statute fixing minimum wages for women exceeded the limits of that power and was unconstitutional and void. The same power justifies an act forbidding the advocating or teaching of the doctrine of resorting to violence as a means of changing industrial and political conditions, but not an act denouncing the display of a red flag as a sign, symbol, or emblem of opposition to organized government.

The equality guaranteed by the final clause of the first section is legal equality, not social equality. In consequence, equality is not denied by state statutes requiring separate railway carriages for the white and colored races or prohibiting the teaching of white and Negro pupils in the same corporate educational institution. Neither is it denied by a statute prohibiting adultery and providing a heavier penalty when the crime is committed by persons of different races than when both guilty parties belong to the same race, nor by the refusal of the managers of a primary (as distinguished from a general) election to permit Negroes to vote therein. On the other hand, an anti-trust statute, imposing fines for unlawful combinations of capital or skill but containing a proviso exempting agricultural products or livestock while in the hands of the producer, is unconstitutional by reason of the inequality resulting from the exemption contained in the proviso; and a municipal ordinance which vests in supervisors the right to grant or withhold their assent to the use of wooden buildings as laundries is likewise unconstitutional as applied to one who has complied with every requisite precaution both for the protection of neighboring property from fire and against injury to the public health.

In each of the cases in which the amendment has been construed, its application to particular states of fact has been declared or denied by the Court, and the rights and obligations of individual litigants have been finally determined. If all these determinations were stated, the result might well be described as the amendment in fact, as distinguished from either intention or theory.

If such an attempt were made we should make an end of speaking about rights and liberties and begin to speak about men and things. We should have to record that the amendment protected Wong Kim Ark, the American-born son of Chinese subjects, when he was refused permission to land at San Francisco on returning to this country from a visit to China, but not John Elk, an American Indian, when he was denied the right to register as a voter in the Fifth Ward of Omaha; the Indianapolis Water Company against the water rates fixed by the Public Service Commission of Indiana, but not the Knoxville Water Company against the water rates fixed by the City of Knoxville; August Bartels against the penalties imposed upon him by an Iowa statute for teaching German to children in a parochial school, but not Albert W. Hamilton against a regulation of the University of California requiring him to take a course in military science and tactics; Yick Wo, a subject of the Emperor of China, when he was imprisoned in San Francisco for engaging in the laundry business in a frame building, but not Soon Hing, also a Chinese subject, when he was imprisoned in the same city for engaging in the laundry business between the hours of ten P.M. and six A.M.; L. A. Nixon, a Negro, when he was prohibited by a

Texas statute from voting in a primary election in that state, but not R. R. Grovey, also a Negro, when he was prohibited by the resolution of a party convention from voting in a similar election in the same state; Joseph Tipaldo when he was indicted for failing to comply with the provisions of the New York Minimum Wage Act, but not West Coast Hotel Company when it was sued by Elsie Parrish, a chambermaid in its employ, for the difference between the wages which she had actually received and the amount to which she was entitled under the provisions of the Washington Minimum Wage Act; and Yetta Stromberg when she directed the children in a summer camp in a ritual which consisted of raising a red flag and pledging allegiance to the cause for which the flag stood, but not Benjamin Gitlow when he arranged for the publication of a manifesto advocating the forcible overthrow of the established political system of the United States.

These illustrations are not given to call attention to any real or supposed conflict in the decisions of the court, but only to emphasize two conclusions which are in any event too plain to be controverted: (1) *In a number of respects the amendment does not mean what its proponents intended.* (2) *In an even greater number of respects it does mean what its proponents never intended. In short, both by way of exclusion and by way of inclusion, the second Fourteenth Amendment is radically different from the first.* The political significance of this antithesis remains to be considered.

3

Hardly anyone any longer denies that judges make law, at least within some definitions of that regrettably elastic word. From what has been said it is clear that they make not only law of the ordinary sort, but also constitutional provisions. The extent of their contribution to a particular article or section depends on the generality of the language of the text, and on the variety and nature of the questions presented for determination in actual litigation. Where the language used is clear and specific, as in the case of the attempt to establish national prohibition by the Eighteenth Amendment, the judicial contribution is comparatively small. On the other hand, where the language of the text is as vague and general as that of the due process clause, the contribution of the judge may well prove even more important than that of the legislative draftsman. It is a gross understatement to say that the representatives who voted for the Fourteenth Amendment did not intend all the consequences which have resulted from its adoption. The simple truth is that most of these consequences were neither considered nor foreseen by anyone, whether representative or elector, at any time during the period in which the adoption of the amendment was discussed. The question before us is how we are to characterize that part of the amendment which has been written by the Supreme Court. The question comes to this: Admitting that judges, though ostensibly only interpreters, make law and make constitutional provisions, what is a "good" law or a "good" constitutional provision, and what is a "bad" one?

There is a school of thought which seeks to make social utility the test of legislative and judicial excellence. If this test is a correct one, we must describe as "good" every interpretation of the amendment, not plainly unreasonable, which was adopted by the Court against an alternative less likely to promote the general welfare; and we must describe as "bad" every interpretation adopted against an alternative not plainly unreasonable and more likely to promote the general welfare. In short, since the Court acts in a sense involuntarily and answers only the questions propounded by particular litigants, "good" and "bad" must sometimes be understood to mean "better" and "worse"; but the standard by which better and worse are to be distinguished is the social advantage or detriment which seems likely to result from the decision announced.

I agree that the field of judicial legislation is limited in the nature of the case by the not unreasonable alternatives between which the Court must choose.[1] I do not agree, however, that these alternatives are to be evaluated on the basis of their social utility. Within the limits stated, the test of lawmaking by courts is no different from that of lawmaking by any other of the instrumentalities by which, in a democracy, the popular will is expressed and enforced. Our theory of government presupposes a representative endowed with common sense—not a mere mouthpiece for the electors who supported him—and a judge learned in the law—neither a creature of the executive on the one hand nor an irresponsible eclectic on the other. The representative is to enact statutes and constitutions, and the judge is to give a reasonable construction to the statutes and constitutions so enacted. Both representative and judge must do honest work in their respective fields if the democratic process is to function properly. In the long run, however, their work must stand or fall not on the ground of social benefit or detriment, but on the accuracy with which it conforms to the dominant forces of usage and opinion. Where no such conformity exists, either the representative or the judge has failed. The elaborate mechanism of democracy has broken down at one point or the other, and has belied the sovereign power which it was called into being to express. "The people," said John Marshall in *Cohens* v. *Virginia*, "made the constitution, and the people can

[1] "I recognize without hesitation that judges do and must legislate, but they can do so only interstitially; they are confined from molar to molecular motions. A common-law judge could not say, 'I think the doctrine of consideration a bit of historical nonsense and shall not enforce it in my court.'" Mr. Justice Holmes in *Southern Pacific Company* v. *Jensen*. In other words, the refusal of the judge to enforce the doctrine would amount to the adoption of an unreasonable alternative.

unmake it. It is the creature of their will, and lives only by their will. But this supreme and irresistible power to make or unmake, resides only in the whole body of the people; not in any subdivision of them."

It must be admitted that the conception of law made by "the whole body of the people" tends to become metaphysical, indeed almost mystical, if carried to its logical limits. According to some of its expositors, the only duty of both representative and judge is to declare the law as it already exists in the mind of the people. Such a theory ignores some of the realities of the legislative process. It would be absurd to argue, for instance, that the recent and useful "lame duck" amendment may be justified only if it was proposed and adopted in response to a popular demand; or that the twenty-six judges who considered in *Di Santo* v. *Pennsylvania* [2] the right of the legislature of Pennsylvania to require the licensing of persons engaged in the sale of steamship tickets might have been guided in their deliberations by a proper responsiveness to the general will on the particular point in controversy. To admit so much is not, however, to say that there is no general will about efficiency in government or about the right of a state to the exercise of the police power.

As was aptly observed by Mr. Justice Holmes, "no one denies that there is a difference between night and day," and

[2] In this extraordinarily close case the Court of Quarter Sessions of Dauphin County, Pennsylvania, which consisted of three members, held that the statute was constitutional. The Superior Court of Pennsylvania held that the statute was unconstitutional and reversed the judgment of the lower court. Two of the seven judges of the Superior Court dissented. The Supreme Court of Pennsylvania, consisting of seven members, held that the statute was constitutional and reversed the judgment of the Superior Court. The Supreme Court of the United States held that the statute was unconstitutional and reversed the judgment of the Supreme Court of Pennsylvania. Three justices dissented. Assuming that the three judges of the Court of Quarter Sessions of Dauphin County, Pennsylvania, were unanimous, a point on which I am without information, fifteen ol the twenty-six judges thought that the statute was constitutional and eleven thought that it was unconstitutional. The case was not decided under the Fourteenth Amendment but under the Commerce Clause.

"the fixing of a point when day ends is made inevitable by the admission of that difference." When only one manufacturer out of a hundred has installed in his factory a given safety device, the device in question is certainly not in customary use. When ninety-nine of the same manufacturers have successively adopted the device, it certainly is in customary use. The admission of this difference makes it necessary to assert that the act of a single manufacturer converted an unusual practice into a usual one. To say that the effective act was that of the fifty-first manufacturer is only to apply a rule of thumb to the solution of a doubtful point. Both law and politics are beset with difficulties of this sort. For present purposes it is sufficient that there are statutes and decisions which represent the popular will, and other statutes and decisions which misrepresent it. The validity of the distinction remains unaffected by the fact that there is a twilight zone in which the attempt to apply it requires determinations which are necessarily arbitrary and sometimes even unreal.

The premises of democracy have been stated by no one more clearly than by George Santayana. He says:

> The practice of English liberty presupposes two things; that all concerned are fundamentally unanimous, and that each has a plastic nature, which he is willing to modify. If fundamental unanimity is lacking and all are not making in the same general direction, there can be no honest coöperation, no satisfying compromise. Every concession, under such circumstances, would be a temporary one, to be retracted at the first favorable moment; it would amount to a mutilation of one's essential nature, a partial surrender of life, liberty, and happiness, tolerable for a time, perhaps, as the lesser of two evils, but involving a perpetual sullen opposition and hatred. To put things to a vote, and to accept unreservedly the decision of the majority, are points essential to the English system; but they would be absurd if fundamental agreement were not presupposed. Every decision that the majority could conceivably arrive at must leave it

still possible for the minority to live and prosper, even if not exactly in the way they wished. Were this not the case, a decision by vote would be as alien a fatality to any minority as the decree of a foreign tyrant, and at every election the right of rebellion would come into play. In a hearty and sound democracy all questions at issue must be minor matters; fundamentals must have been silently agreed upon and taken for granted when the democracy arose. To leave a decision to the majority is like leaving it to chance—a fatal procedure unless one is willing to have it either way. You must be able to risk losing the toss; and if you do you will acquiesce all the more readily in the result, because unless the winners cheated at the game, they had no more influence on it than yourself—namely none, or very little. You acquiesce in democracy on the same conditions and for the same reasons, and perhaps a little more cheerfully, because there is an infinitesimally better chance of winning on the average; but even then the enormity of the risk involved would be intolerable if anything of vital importance was at stake.

It is easy to set down some of the fundamental unanimities upon which our American polity depends. We are all agreed, for example, that government is better than anarchy and that a democracy is a better form of government than either a monarchy or an aristocracy; that a system of private property is to be preferred to communism; that church and state should be completely separated; that accused persons should be tried in accordance with the traditions of English liberty; that monogamy is the best form of the marriage relation; and that freedom of speech and of the press is one of the essential rights of citizenship. All of these convictions are expressed in the laws of every state of the Union. Most of them are also expressed, in whole or in part, in the Constitution of the United States. Yet all of them have been rejected in one country or another during the course of recorded history, and some of them are rejected today in countries as highly civilized as our own.

To take a single illustration out of many available, the framers of our Constitution wrote into it a provision that no religious test should ever be required as a qualification to any office or public trust under the United States. The article in question is declaratory of a customary point of view by which the religious opinions of public officials are not regarded as matters of vital political importance. If Alfred E. Smith had been elected President, a large body of citizens would doubtless have been displeased, but I do not suppose that any experienced observer believes that a rebellion would have occurred. In Ireland, however, where the memory of old wrongs makes it as intolerable for Catholics to be governed by Protestants as for Protestants to be governed by Catholics, a decision by vote becomes, as Santayana says, "an alien fatality" by which it is known in advance that the minority will refuse to be bound. The difference has nothing to do with relative degrees of civilization or national enlightenment. It results rather from the almost universal acceptance in the United States of an attitude toward religious issues which is not accepted in Ireland. This attitude is the cause rather than the effect of our constitutional provision. The fundamental agreement which democracy presupposes must exist in fact before popular lawmaking becomes a working possibility.

If the people set up constitutional provisions, they also strike them down. When the great Chief Justice spoke of the supreme and irresistible power by which constitutions are unmade, he might well have cited *Chisholm* v. *Georgia* in illustration of his statement. In that case the Court over which he was afterwards called to preside had decided that the judicial power of the United States extended to a suit brought against a state by a citizen of another state. The decision—which would perhaps attract little attention today—proved to be at variance with the spirit of the age in which it was rendered.

In less than five years the supreme and irresistible power had declared by the adoption of the Eleventh Amendment that the Constitution should not be construed in the way in which the Court had construed it. In a somewhat similar way the decision in *Pollock* v. *Farmers Loan and Trust Company*, which denied to Congress the power to impose an income tax, was set aside by the adoption of the Sixteenth Amendment. The Fifteenth Amendment has been virtually nullified in the only part of the country in which its provisions were of any moment. The Eighteenth Amendment, which in my opinion never represented customary morality, was repealed by the Twenty-first Amendment. The Dred Scott decision was overthrown on the battlefields of the Civil War. Mr. Benét has stated one of the plainest facts in our constitutional history, in language which oddly echoes that of John Marshall:

> Sometimes an image that has stood so long
> It seems implanted as the polar star
> Is moved against by an unfathomed force
> That suddenly will not have it any more.
> Call it the mores, call it God or Fate,
> Call it Mansoul or economic law,
> That force exists and moves.

I have suggested the canons of criticism by which I think the decisions under the Fourteenth Amendment ought to be evaluated. The preamble of the Constitution is in the first person plural. The theory behind the grammar seems to me on the whole to correspond to a political reality. On the affirmative side, the mores tend to write our fundamental unanimities into the law of the land. On the negative side, legislation, whether formal or judicial, which proves offensive to the mores, is set aside after one fashion or another—by amendment or repeal, by judicial interpretation or reinterpretation, by nullification or by force—and ceases to be the law of the land. Both sorts of legislation partake, though in varying degrees, of the interstitial character to which Mr. Justice Holmes has referred.[3] The molecular motions of the judge are confined within the intervals of the text which he is called upon to expound. The molar motions of the legislator are likewise confined, though within the larger and vaguer intervals of the usage and opinion which he is chosen to render articulate.

It has been shown that the interpretation of the Fourteenth Amendment has defeated many of the purposes which its proponents intended, and has accomplished other purposes which nobody intended. Neither of these statements necessarily amounts to an indictment of the Court.

On the first point it should be remembered that the amendment was proposed before the passions arising from the Civil War had had time to cool, and that it was adopted at the instance of a "subdivision" of the people, to make use of Marshall's word, against the bitter opposition of a defeated but unreconciled minority. Unlike most articles of the Constitution, its prohibitions were not directed against action by the National Government but against action by the states. These prohibitions might have been so construed as to destroy the essential characteristics of our dual form of government and to impose social equality between the white and black races on the white inhabitants of the South. Without attempting to justify all the decisions of the Court, I venture the opinion that the judges who refused to construe the amend-

[3] The saying that a common-law judge could not refuse to enforce the doctrine of consideration because he happened to regard it as a piece of historical nonsense is the statement of a standard of judicial self-restraint. If the judge did refuse to enforce the doctrine, he would be a bad judge and his view of the law would not ultimately prevail. Within much wider limits, the products of formal legislation are subjected to the same sort of practical revision. That this revision actually takes place is a commonplace of politics. The so-called legal realism which can find law only in the latest decision of the latest controversy seems to me a truism from one point of view and grossly unrealistic from any other.

ment in this way more truly expressed the considered judgment of "the whole body of the people" than did Thaddeus Stevens and the so-called radical Republicans.

The unintended consequences of the amendment have resulted in part from the very nature of a constitution. Herbert Spencer defined life as "the continuous adjustment of internal relations to external relations." When the adjustment ceases to exist, the man is dead. When a constitution can no longer be adjusted to meet the needs of a changing world, the constitution is dead.

> I speak first of the Constitution [says Mr. Justice Cardozo] and in particular of the great immunities with which it surrounds the individual. No one shall be deprived of liberty without due process of law. Here is a concept of the greatest generality. Yet it is put before the courts *en bloc*. Liberty is not defined. Its limits are not mapped and charted. How shall they be known? Does liberty mean the same thing for successive generations? May restraints that were arbitrary yesterday be useful and rational and therefore lawful today? May restraints that are arbitrary today become useful and rational and therefore lawful tomorrow? I have no doubt that the answer to these questions must be yes. . . . The content of constitutional immunities is not constant, but varies from age to age. "The needs of successive generations may make restrictions imperative today, which were vain and capricious to the vision of times past." "We must never forget," in Marshall's mighty phrase, "that it is a *constitution* we are expounding." Statutes are designed to meet the fugitive exigencies of the hour. Amendment is easy as the exigencies change. In such cases, the meaning, once construed, tends legitimately to stereotype itself in the form first cast. A constitution states or ought to state not rules for the passing hour, but principles for an expanding future. In so far as it deviates from that standard and descends into details and particulars, it loses its flexibility, the scope of interpretation contracts, the meaning hardens. While it is true to its function, it maintains its power of adaptation, its suppleness, its play.

We are not to conclude, therefore, that the extension of the Fourteenth Amendment to subjects not considered in the generation in which it was adopted amounts, in itself, to an abuse of the judicial function. I will give two illustrations from decisions which have been widely discussed. Since I regard one of them as good and the other as bad, and since the effect of both was to limit the power of the states, it is apparent that if I approach the questions adjudicated in a spirit of prejudice, the prejudice is not concerned with the subject of states' rights.

I think *Adkins* v. *Children's Hospital*, which denied to the states the power to pass minimum wage laws, was a bad decision and that it was properly overruled in *West Coast Hotel Co.* v. *Parrish.* Both decisions were approved by only a bare majority of the Court, and we may accordingly assume that neither of the alternatives presented was legally unreasonable. I do not characterize the Adkins decision as bad because the subject of minimum wage laws was not considered by the framers of the due process clause, or because I personally regard such laws as desirable, or even because I think most Americans regard them as desirable. I characterize the decision as bad because I think most Americans believe that the states should not be hampered in making experiments intended to promote public health and social security.

I think *Stromberg* v. *California*, by which freedom of speech and of the press was definitely placed beside freedom of contract among the liberties protected by the due process clause, was a good decision. I might easily be brought to share the doubts more than once expressed by Mr. Justice Brandeis about the correctness of the earlier decisions which extended the language of the clause beyond procedural matters. The extension has been made, however, and has met with universal acquiescence, if not with universal approval. Here again I am not concerned with the intention of the framers or with the meaning which they attached to the word "liberty." I characterize the Stromberg decision as good because I think most Americans believe that freedom of speech and of the press is as much a liberty as freedom of contract.

In stating these conclusions I am attempting to determine the will of the sovereign power which made the Constitution yesterday and can unmake it tomorrow, whose effects have been identified in the moving forces of usage and opinion and which has been variously referred to as the mores and the spirit of the times. Mr. Justice Cardozo has noted regretfully that "in every court there are likely to be as many estimates of the *Zeitgeist* as there are judges on its bench." I understand this saying to mean no more than that it is hard to be a good judge. I may be mistaken about what the will of the sovereign is. But if I am also mistaken about the source of sovereignty, I am persuaded that there is no meaning in democracy.

VIII

TWO SINS AGAINST TOLERANCE

In a catechism which I used to study there was a classification of sins on the basis of virtues in the somewhat discouraging ratio of two to one. The path of godliness, it appeared, was beset with temptations on either side. One could have too much or too little of the quality of every virtue, but whether one sinned by way of excess or by way of deficiency one was equally far from being in a state of grace. Thus it was said that the sins against Hope were Presumption on the one hand and Despair on the other.

I hold no brief either for or against such a method of classification as a piece of abstract casuistry, but I am interested in its present application to the theory and practice of Tolerance, which is the newest and therefore the least generally understood of the cardinal virtues. Moreover, at the risk of seeming unduly dogmatic, I am willing to assert that the sins against Tolerance are Skepticism and Bigotry, and that, paradoxical as it may seem, we Americans are simultaneously in danger of becoming skeptics as a matter of philosophy and bigots as a matter of fact.

1

The roots of skepticism lie in the very general modern acceptance of what I have come to regard as one of the most pernicious heresies under the sun—the doctrine, namely, that truth and error are subjective matters which rest on nothing more enduring than personal opinion and which have no relation to objective reality. I am not attacking the teachings of any formal school of philosophy. I am only trying to express the attitude of most of the people who think of themselves and speak of themselves as liberals. Go into any church which calls itself liberal or advanced, and you will be told in substance that it is not necessary to be right but only to think that you are right.

This is not only a very soft doctrine, but it is softer than the facts. Upon the very fabric of life is stamped the stern command that you must be right at your peril. Not for nothing was it written that it must needs be that offenses come, but woe to that man by whom the offense cometh. To say that polygamy is a meritorious practice for Mormons because they honestly believe in it is to say that the world was flat before Columbus proved that it was round. To say that Democrats and Republicans are equally patriotic is to state a perfectly evident fact, but to say that their political opinions are equally sound is to state an absurdity. Moreover, it is an absurdity which no one is so foolish as to commit in practical affairs. No one for a moment supposes that a clear conscience will heat a cold room or turn a bad meal into a good one. We live our lives subject to rigorous physical laws, and when we violate them we take the consequences. What we are to eat and how we are to live are questions which we are bound to answer at our own risk. If we fail to answer them correctly, mere goodness of intention will not help us a whit.

Much good work has been done in recent years in the field of prison reform, but some of it has been marred by a failure to remember that a prisoner is, after all, a man who has committed a crime. It is utterly beside the point to answer that if we knew all we should forgive all. There is respectable authority for the proposition that it is our duty to forgive all whether we know all or not. God alone can measure the length and breadth of human sin in the light of his infinite mercy. But neither our knowledge nor our forgiveness is any reason, so far as I can see, for supposing that a murderer is any the less a murderer because he has added unwritten amendments to the text of the Ten Commandments. It is precisely the case of the man who is out of step with the regiment. As a piece of pure logic, it is possible (though unlikely) that the man and the regiment are both out of step with the music. But it is unthinkable that they are both in step with it, and at the same time out of step with each other.

Nor do I think that any more can be said on behalf of this particular kind of liberalism if we pass altogether outside the field of individual ethics. It is generally conceded, for instance, that the Civil War was the most tremendous domestic crisis through which America has passed up to the present time. Every mind indignantly rejects the idea that sin can in any wise be imputed to the men who faced each other on the battlefields of that war. We are humbly conscious rather that their conduct was equally above all praise. And yet it is a mockery, which they would be the first to resent, to suggest that the cause which prevailed was neither better nor worse than the one which was defeated.

Another national crisis is upon us today. As I write these words, a battle is being waged, behind the rights and wrongs of puzzling specific instances, between those who are seeking to fulfill and those others, whether fascist or communist, who are seeking to destroy, the social and political hopes and aspirations to which the American Commonwealth was dedicated. In the issue thus joined it is altogether likely that each side honestly believes in the justice and wisdom of its cause. It is certain, however, that one side or the other is mistaken, and neither idealism, however unselfish, nor loyalty, however devoted, can abate the awful consequences of that certainty. Let our citizens look to it—the welfare of their children will depend on the course which they adopt and not on the purity of the motives which may lead to its adoption.

It must be admitted, of course, that truth is one thing and our idea of it another; but this is only the tacit admission behind every human affirmation. If we never spoke except upon certain knowledge, we should always be silent. "A decent respect to the opinions of mankind" bids us beware of a wayward cocksureness; but pure skepticism implies an indecent disrespect to our own opinions, which is one of the clearest of the stigmata of decadence. It was the disciples of Pyrrho and not of Socrates who doubted whether they doubted. Our forefathers professed "a decent respect to the opinions of mankind," but they nevertheless had no scruples about pitching several thousand pounds of tea into Boston harbor. They also hanged witches at Salem, and did many other fierce and wrong acts; but they never committed the sin of Pontius Pilate, whose name has been detestable for two thousand years, because, at a stupendous crisis, he could do no better than to ask, "What is truth?"

I have a friend, a lawyer, who has frequently had occasion to examine two medical experts as witnesses on his side of various important cases. The physicians in question are in all respects equally distinguished practitioners, but my friend considers one of them a much safer witness than the other. He bases this belief on the answer which each is accustomed to make to a usual question in the course of cross-examination. This question is whether the witness may not be mistaken in his opinion. The first physician always says, "Certainly," without more. The second replies, "I may be mistaken, *but I think not*"; and my friend is satisfied that the emphasis on the added words carries great weight with juries.

Logically, the second answer is a piece of tautology, because in stating any opinion one necessarily expresses a belief in its correctness; but the tautology springs from unfairness inherent in the question itself. An admission of possible error is the unspoken preface of every speech. Fallibility is the inertia against which a man moves when he undertakes to speak at all. How positively he may be justified in speaking depends upon "an assemblage of probabilities" of which he must be the judge. This "assemblage of probabilities" may be so strong as to amount to a moral certainty, or so weak as to make the adherence to a judgment based upon it mere stubbornness. In either case tolerance certainly demands nothing so absurd as a concession that one opinion is as good as another because both may be wrong.

Now tolerance is a by-product of democracy, professing the the same doctrine and subject to the same limitations. The essence of democracy is not equality, but equality before the law. The essence of tolerance is not doubt, but charity and a sense of fair play. The vice of the bigot and the despot is not certitude, but a refusal to hear both sides of the case. Freedom of thought no more implies an approval of heresy than freedom of action implies an approval of crime. Everyone has a right to a hearing, just as everyone has a right to a chance in the world; but truth and worth are, none the less, solemn and detached realities which nothing can controvert.

All this is, in a sense, a protest against a modern point of view. In another sense it is a personal profession of faith. The objective distinction between good and evil, and our fitness to make that distinction, seem to me first principles which increase in importance with our own perplexities. If the world is indeed a wilderness, it is both untrue and foolish to keep repeating that all paths lead straight to the broad highway; and it is equally foolish to follow only half-heartedly what seems to us the best path, for the reason that our neighbor may possibly have hit upon a better one. There is no way out of the labyrinth except to find the clue. Nothing will discharge our obligation to find it except performance. On such a theory, life is a perilous quest which may end in achievement. On any other, it is a meaningless nightmare without an end in view. It was Shakespeare who wrote, "for there is nothing either good or bad but thinking makes it so."

But it is worth remembering that he put these words in the mouth of Hamlet, who was either a madman or a sane man successfully feigning madness, as the critics may prefer.

2

But if the sin of skepticism lies in a perversion of liberal thinking, the menace of bigotry is chiefly to be found in an equally dangerous perversion of conservative conduct and leadership.

The American people are just now confronted with the wave of social and political unrest which has been sweeping over the world since the end of the World War. It is, I suppose, impossible to approach the questions which are now before us for consideration without some mental predisposition one way or the other. In approaching them I am aware that my own predisposition, both innately and as a matter of training, must be described as conservative, unless the meaning of that word has lost all relation to its etymology. I really believe, for instance, that a democracy is a more desirable form of state than either a monarchy or an aristocracy, and I desire to preserve what seem to me the essentials of the particular form of democracy which our forefathers established. I am as far as possible from being a fascist, a communist, or an anarchist. I believe in an economic system founded on private property and in an industrial system supported by private capital and conducted by private initiative. I am opposed to any change in the established distribution of powers among the executive, the legislative, and the judicial branches of our government.

These are simply my own conclusions, which may be quite incorrect as a matter of fact, though, like my friend's witness, *I think not*. But, so far as my fellow citizens are concerned, my conclusions are, in a certain sense at least, entirely irrelevant.

They are part of a composite judgment, nothing more, and they are entitled to only so much weight as their own intrinsic worth, backed by the weight of my personal authority, be that much or little, is able to win for them. "All power," says the Constitution of my own state, in words which fairly express the political philosophy underlying the Constitution of the United States as well, "is inherent in the people and all free governments are founded on their authority and instituted for their peace, safety and happiness. For the advancement of these ends they have at all times an inalienable and indefeasible right to alter, reform or abolish their government in such manner as they may think proper."

But the right thus stated is, in the United States, happily more than the abstract product of any paper constitution. It is a perfectly practical fact, and every American knows it. Whenever a substantial majority of our fellow citizens, having soberly considered both sides of the case, desires to adopt the social and political theories of Stalin or Hitler, it not only has a theoretical right so to do, but it has, by means of constitutional amendments, the actual power to accomplish such a result. Precisely because this is the case, the right of free speech, even as its warmest advocates have defined it, affords no protection to the agitator whose words create a clear and present danger of an attempt to overthrow by force our present form of government. The crime for which such an agitator may be indicted is of statutory origin, but logically it is treason —not treason against the United States in the technical sense, but treason against the basic principle of democracy, which is that the will of the whole people (provisionally determined from day to day by the instrumentality of the ballot) is paramount to the will of any part of the people.

Now, if it be true that the people have a right "to alter, reform or abolish" their government at will—and we Americans should be the last to dispute it—and, further, if it be true that it is here and now treason against democracy and tolerance for a minority, either radical or reactionary, to attempt the forcible overthrow of a political order with which they happen to disagree, it is equally—and for the same reasons—treason against democracy and tolerance for a conservative majority forcibly to prevent a full and free discussion of the views of political thinkers with whom they happen to disagree. Indeed, one proposition necessarily depends on the other. Revolution by force is a crime only when revolution by argument and persuasion is an ever present possibility. Free speech is not merely one of the results of democracy; it is likewise one of the continuing causes of democracy. When free speech ceases, public opinion ceases; and when the rule of public opinion ceases, despotism begins. The American tradition affirms that the forcible overthrow of despotism is not base but noble.

Not long ago a well-known clergyman and educator delivered a public lecture in the city in which I live. In the course of his remarks he said that if he were President of the United States he would order the arrest of every communist in the country, would have them taken to New York harbor, and thence "on a ship of stone with sails of lead" would "start them straight for the closest port of Hell." The speaker was an educated native-born citizen and was speaking in a small and thoroughly American inland city, but one seldom hears more seditious language on the lips of an illiterate immigrant haranguing foreigners in the heart of one of our great centers of population. In principle such an utterance is quite as bad as that for which the so-called criminal anarchist may be sent (as I think rightly) to jail. In practice it is a great deal more sinister and alarming. The number of radical agitators in the United States is said to be about twenty thousand. The number of influential conservatives is many times as great.

It is, therefore, chiefly upon the temperance and fortitude of conservative leadership that the safety of America depends.

I have said that I have faith in our political institutions. I have faith in our people as well. "It is not uninteresting to the world," said Thomas Jefferson, "that an experiment should be fairly and fully made whether freedom of discussion, unaided by power, is not sufficient for the propagation and protection of truth." We find ourselves in the midst of this experiment, and I for one am willing to engage in debate with the apostles of the totalitarian state, not only because tolerance entitles both sides to a hearing, but because I believe I have a better case than they have and because I have confidence in the court and jury.

The Constitution of the United States can claim for itself none of the sacred character which the Hebrews attributed to the laws of Moses. It was devised by wise and patriotic men after a score of compromises. It was adopted after the most unrestricted consideration in the forum of public opinion. It stands vindicated in the record of a century and a half of progress and development without a parallel in the history of civilization. If, then, the form of government which the Constitution set up cannot now win for itself vindication as a working success from the same tribunal which approved it as a mere experiment, the obvious conclusion would seem to be that our government is not really so good as I think it is—in other words, that my own conclusion on this point is quite wrong. In that case we ought by all means to avail ourselves of the first opportunity to replace our present political structure by a better one.

There is only one other possible point of view, and that is that the people are incompetent to select their own form of government. If that is true, democracy has failed; and if democracy has failed, America has failed. Personally

I have no fear on this point, but even if I had, being an American and remembering the aspirations, the self-denial, the blood and tears, the anguish and longing that have gone into the making of America—it seems to me that I would at least give democracy the benefit of the doubt and continue, albeit with a waning faith, along the old paths, even as Peter, though he denied his Lord, nevertheless "followed afar off . . . to see the end."

IX

AN OPEN LETTER TO THE CONSERVATIVE MAJORITY

A CONSERVATIVE is one who seeks to preserve the existing order; a progressive, one who seeks to improve it; a reactionary, one who seeks to destroy it in order to restore an earlier order; and a radical, one who seeks to destroy it in order to make a new beginning. If any reader is disposed to quarrel with these definitions, let him accept them tentatively and for present purposes only. Assuming this done, it immediately becomes necessary to make two preliminary observations.

In the first place, it must be apparent that the points of view which I have denominated conservative, progressive, reactionary, and radical are in themselves quite without ethical significance. By their fruits they are to be known and judged. Abraham Lincoln and Nicholas II were both conservatives; if the world will long remember the President and will forget the Czar, the reason lies, at least in part, in the judgment of history that the American Union was better worth saving than Holy Russia. The despotism of Louis XIV was as progressive a development of the power of the French kings as was the glorious Revolution of that of the English Parliament; if we prefer the latter to the former, we do so because we are accustomed to set more store by the rights of man than by efficiency in government. Joan of Arc, the peasant girl who freed France, and Napoleon III, the Emperor who enslaved her, were equally reactionary. The logic of events made the signing of the Declaration of Independence as radical an act as the storming of the Bastile; but the American Revolution was followed by the Constitutional Convention of 1787, and the French Revolution was followed by the Reign of Terror and the despotism of the First Empire. It is, after all, the quality of the things which men seek to preserve, to develop, to restore, or to build anew that justifies or condemns their conduct.

In the second place, it must be apparent that of the four attitudes under consideration the conservative and the progressive have at least this in common, that they depend on a faith in the continuity of human history and experience; and the reactionary and the radical have at least this in common, that they spring from a complete dissatisfaction with things as they are. Of course a man may be simultaneously a conservative or a progressive in one connection and a reactionary or a radical in another, but it is still true that in any given connection the difference between a conservative and a progressive is simply a matter of emphasis, and the difference between a reactionary and a radical is simply a matter of opinion as to what ought to be done after the status quo has been destroyed.

As everyone knows, both reaction and radicalism are abroad in the world at the present time. How much of either actually exists in the United States is perhaps a debatable point, but at any rate there is, here as elsewhere, a great hue and cry about them. In its extreme form this agitation is expressed in statements to the effect that in the long run America is certain to become either fascist or communist, and that the only issue for our citizens to decide is which of the two alternatives to adopt. Most Americans find one horn of the dilemma as piercing as the other. The consequence is that the preservation of our form of government seems to them for the time being even more important than its improvement. It is to the conservative majority thus constituted that the following communication is addressed.

1

At the outset I ought to say that I write as one of you. The ancient Greeks were better philosophers than we Americans are and, man for man, were better men. The Romans were better law-givers. The Hebrews were more religious. The Germans are certainly more painstaking and possibly more profound. But we belong—at least by virtue of our political traditions—to the Anglo-Saxon race, and the Anglo-Saxon race has made a unique contribution to the accumulated wisdom of the world, viz., the development of a special sort of democracy which is exemplified in the system of government which our fathers set up in the United States. We agree in believing that this system of government is, all in all, eminently worth preserving.

But in politics, as in war, it is a great deal easier to attack than to defend. Some of us have forgotten exactly what it is in our institutions that we have reason to be grateful for, just as children sometimes forget what they are crying about, though keeping none the less a sense of having been wronged. And so our replies to the attacks of both reactionaries and radicals have often been confused and stupid. Among other things, we have sometimes answered the charge that our government was all wrong in such a way as to suggest that we believe it to be all right. We are likely to fare badly in any argument joined on such an issue, because of course it is not all right, and as soon as we attempt to prove that it is we are bound to get into all sorts of difficulties. In point of fact it is full of defects and inequalities, but our reply to our adversaries ought to be simply that it is better, both in theory and in practice, than any substitute they have to offer, and that it can be made better still. That is part of our task today; in a plainer sense it will be the task of our children tomorrow. We know, however, that they cannot build that City of God of which the fathers dreamed unless we transmit to them uninjured the foundation upon which its superstructure is to stand.

But it is not only in debate that we have been forgetful and stupid. Let me illustrate what I mean by referring to events with which most of us are entirely familiar. Not long after the end of the World War the Assembly of the State of New York refused on two occasions to seat duly elected representatives of the Socialist Party, solely because they were Socialists. Much more recently, in 1935, the Congress of the United States adopted virtually without debate or dissent the so-called "Red rider," under the official construction of which no teacher in the public schools of the District of Columbia might discuss, even in his own home, the theory or practice of Communism without forfeiting his salary as a teacher. More recently still Earl Browder was arrested and prevented from speaking in Terre Haute while campaigning for the Presidency of the United States on the Communist ticket. These things were done in the name of Americanism—that is, in our name as conservatives—and by agencies of our government itself, so that it seemed as if they were the fruits of the very system which we are seeking to preserve. I say "seemed," because in the narrow sense in which I am now using the word our government changes from year to year, almost from day to day, and these particular acts were committed by groups of men who had been placed in power directly or indirectly by us and could have been removed by us as soon as their terms of office expired. But to unthinking persons such a distinction was by no means obvious.

Now in this state of affairs it is perfectly clear, for several reasons, that the cause of the radicals was not really menaced at all. In the first place, all history bears witness to the truth of what was wittily observed by Mr. Justice Holmes in declining during the Prohibition era an invitation to discuss the subject, "Freedom of Speech," that "with effervescing opinions, as with the not yet forgotten champagnes, the quickest way to let them get flat is to let them be exposed to the air." The Czars of Russia deported all the radicals they could lay their hands on for five hundred years. It might seem in consequence that at the end of that period there would have been no radicals left in Russia. But the facts show that there were, unhappily, almost no conservatives left in Russia.

Furthermore, the position of the radicals was strengthened rather than weakened by repression, because the very fact of repression gave color to their repeated and continued assertion that the existence of a free popular government in the United States is more apparent than real. When a man says that his government is not free, and is immediately persecuted—or seems to be persecuted—for saying so, it looks very much on the face of things as if he were right in his contention.

Finally, the success of the radicals was not jeopardized by any of the acts of which we are speaking, because these acts, though done in our name, were thoroughly reactionary in character. The things which were jeopardized by them were representative government in the first instance cited, and civil liberty in the second and third. Now representative government and civil liberty are inextricably bound up with the political ideals and traditions of the United States. Our ancestors have cherished them on two continents and for almost a thousand years. If they were to be struck out of the framework of our government, there would be an end of that government as we now know it. In brief, there would be an end of the existing political order. But the radicals had nothing to fear on that account, because the destruction of the existing order is, as we have seen, the one aim which is held by reactionaries and radicals alike.

In view of all these considerations, it would have been very good tactics on our part—to say nothing of anything else—to go to the defense of the radicals with all the strength we had. If we had done so, we could have stopped the forces of reaction almost at the outset, and our cause would have gained the immense credit of defeating a menace quite as revolutionary as that of communism. It is gratifying to remember that some of our leaders and representatives did speak out, and speak out plainly. But too many of us were guilty of the incredible folly of sitting idly by, while a radical minority, many of whom were not native-born Americans and some of whom were not Americans at all, fought the battle of Americanism for us. In so far as they won it, we may rejoice with all our hearts at the result, but it is impossible not to feel that our own authority has been tremendously discredited. Moreover, the nature of the case makes complete reparation impossible. The "Red rider" has been repealed, but as Mr. Grenville Clark has forcibly pointed out,[1] no act of legislation or decree of court can compensate Mr. Browder for the loss of his right to speak on the particular day on which his right was denied.

2

I have said that the justification of our point of view in present-day politics is to be found in the fact that the institutions of the United States exemplify a special and unique sort of democracy, and further that representative government and civil liberty are inextricably bound up with these institutions. Such a statement falls short of the whole truth of the matter. Representative government and civil liberty are more than necessary incidentals of that form of democracy which exists in the United States. They are in themselves the very essentials of its significance and uniqueness. In them is summed up the whole of our contribution to what the world has learned about the science of politics. The Greeks knew something about the despotism of majorities, if that be democracy, and the Germans know something about obedience to law, if that be liberty. But neither the Greeks nor the Germans nor any other people have understood representative

[1] "Constitutional Rights," Pamphlet Series, No. 6, The American Academy of Political and Social Science, Philadelphia, 1938.

government and civil liberty as we have understood them. Without them experience teaches that no democracy can succeed. Our fathers had faith to believe that with them our own could not fail. We conservatives have professed, at least with our lips, the faith of our fathers.

But if representative government and civil liberty are the objects of our peculiar care, they have no place in the programs of our adversaries. "Fascism," says Mussolini, "combats the whole complex system of democratic ideology, and repudiates it, whether in its theoretical premises or in its practical application. . . . We solemnly bury that lie—democratic universal suffrage. We do not care a damn for this public opinion." "The working class," says Trotsky, "cannot guarantee the democratic character of its dictatorship without transgressing the limits of its democratic program." "The syndicalist," says Mr. A. D. Lewis in *Syndicalism and the General Strike*, "has a contempt for the vulgar idea of democracy; the vast unconscious mass is not to be taken into account when the minority wishes to act so as to benefit it."

Language such as this, which at least has the merits of clearness and candor, leaves nothing at issue between the fascist and the communist except the method of determining the things which are likely to prove beneficial to the "vast unconscious mass"—in any case the views of the mass are not to be considered at all. On the other hand, democracy cannot survive except for the existence of a public opinion which is enlightened as well as governing. It is the office of civil liberty to create such a public opinion, and that of representative government to express it. If we accepted the premises of Mr. Browder, there could be no logical objection to our putting him and all of his followers in jail. Doubtless it is what they would do to us if the destinies of the American people were in their hands and circumstances made such a course seem expedient. But the destinies of the American people are in our hands. Just here we come, definitely and finally, to the parting of the ways.

For it is manifest that an obligation rests upon us which depends on considerations much deeper than expediency and more compelling than an abstract sense of fair play—an obligation, moreover, by which we alone are bound and which differs in kind from any assumed by our opponents. We must protect free institutions at the peril of everything else, because free institutions are the fundamentals of our own case in chief. Without them our cause cannot prosper or even endure. To compass or permit their abridgment in the the name of saving democracy is suicidal, because it cuts away the foundation on which democracy stands. It is, politically speaking, the sin against the Holy Ghost—democracy denying itself. A fascist and a communist ought to be liberals perhaps, but a democrat must be one.

When, therefore, those who would persuade us to change our form of government have been silenced without due process of law, they have suffered nothing but the personal inconvenience of imprisonment or discrimination. But we have suffered the moral consequences of apostasy. Due process of law is our phrase and not theirs. It is we who have hitherto asserted the principles which make for free speech and a free press, and they who have denied them. When the Socialists walked out of the New York Assembly, they had lost nothing but their seats. But we had lost, in that particular connection, a part of our birthright. It is we and not they who have quoted with pride the saying that taxation without representation is tyranny. If Mr. Browder can persuade a majority of our fellow citizens to adopt the tenets of communism, no man knows, indeed, what the result will be. But we have one abiding comfort—whatever it is, it will not be communism according to his definition and it will be democracy according to ours.

All this is neither visionary nor unduly optimistic. It is not visionary because it is only a restatement of the axioms which underlie every noteworthy political achievement of the Anglo-Saxon race from Magna Carta to the Constitution of the United States. And it is no more optimistic than democracy itself. If the success of our government depends on the ability of the people to govern themselves, it is surely a very simple thing to say that we, who have risked everything on that supposition, ought reasonably to act as if we had faith in it. For faith, as has been finely said, "is, on the practical side, just the resolution to stand or fall by the noblest hypothesis," and without faith no hypothesis, even though it be true in fact, is worth anything in practical affairs. The human body is really lighter than water, but that fact will not help a man who is out of his depth and insists on trying to walk—he must act as if he believed in the laws of physics before the laws of physics will help him. In like manner, if we wish to justify democracy, it is of first importance that we give democracy a chance to justify itself.

But is our hypothesis true in fact? I have assumed its truth from the outset, because I have been writing as a conservative to conservatives, and such an assumption is, after all, our only reason for being what we are. And yet the question is an important one, though the issue is not in our keeping. As surely as no act of the swimmer could change the inevitable result if the laws of gravity were against him instead of being in his favor, so surely the deluge impends if the premises of democracy are ill founded.

Our fathers have proved some of them to be true. And how about those which remain to be proved by us and by our children? Well, they still constitute, as it seems to me, the noblest hypothesis. For democracy implies more than the fitness of the people to govern themselves. It presupposes a world in which truth, if let alone, will in the end prevail over error, and righteousness be vindicated. Some of you will remember the words of Gamaliel. He was speaking of men who taught what seemed to be so revolutionary a doctrine that certain of their countrymen took counsel to slay them. "Take heed to yourselves," he said, "what ye intend to do as touching these men. For before these days rose up Theudas, boasting himself to be somebody; to whom a number of men, about four hundred, joined themselves; who was slain; and all, as many as obeyed him, were scattered, and brought to naught. After this man rose up Judas of Galilee in the days of the taxing, and drew away many people after him; he also perished; and all, even as many as obeyed him, were dispersed. And now I say unto you, Refrain from these men and let them alone; for if this counsel or this work be of men, it will come to naught; but if it be of God, ye cannot overthrow it; lest haply ye be found to fight even against God." The men to whom he referred were progressives rather than radicals, because they spoke in the name of One who said that He came not to destroy but to fulfil. In the fullness of time it was their cause before which "the prejudices of the Synagogue, and the doubts of the Academy, and the pride of the portico, and the fasces of the Lictor and the swords of thirty legions were humbled in the dust." Gamaliel was a conservative. The fact that he was a conservative at that particular time and place shows that he lacked vision. But he was a good democrat for all that, and his doctrine is our doctrine.

X

A BRIEF ON THE PLAY SCENE

THE recent trilogy of Professor J. Dover Wilson [1] has served to direct attention anew to the subject of *Hamlet* and particularly to the play scene, which Professor Wilson correctly regards as "the climax and crisis of the whole drama." In the course of his elaborate reconstruction of this scene he comes face to face with the problem of the identification of the "speech of some dozen or sixteen lines" which Hamlet undertook to "set down and insert" in *The Murder of Gonzago*, a play already in the repertory of the strolling players. As every reader of Shakespeare will remember, the avowed objects of Hamlet in having the play produced were to test the honesty of the Ghost, and, if that were established, to "catch the conscience of the King." In explaining his plan to Horatio immediately before the performance began he said that one scene came "near the circumstance" of his father's death as narrated by the Ghost, and added that if the King's "occulted guilt" did not "itself unkennel in *one speech*" he was prepared to regard the Ghost as an impostor from Hell instead of the spirit of his father. When the play was presented the King rose in terror when Lucianus, the Player-Murderer, poured the mock poison in the Player-King's ears. Thereupon, on the order of Polonius, the play was abandoned in the middle of a scene and with Lucianus still on the stage.

Professor Wilson concedes that the identification of Hamlet's lines presents a vexed question "over which much paper and ink have been expended." An examination of the notes in the Furness Variorum edition of *Hamlet* abundantly justifies this statement. According to one opinion, the lines are contained in the long and moralizing speech of the Player-King which immediately follows the gratuitous promise of his con-

[1] *Hamlet, The Manuscript of Shakespeare's Hamlet,* and *What Happens in Hamlet.*

sort not to remarry in the event of his death. On the other hand, much support may be found for the conclusion adopted by Professor Wilson that the inserted speech is the one spoken by Lucianus at the moment when the play murder is committed. The purposes of this paper are to show that both conclusions are mistaken; to advance as the true explanation that the performance of the play was interrupted before Hamlet's speech had been delivered; and, finally, to suggest what the subject of the missing speech was.

The lines of Lucianus selected by Professor Wilson are as follows:

> Thoughts black, hands apt, drugs fit, and time agreeing,
> Confederate season, else no creature seeing,
> Thou mixture rank, of midnight weeds collected,
> With Hecate's ban thrice blasted, thrice infected,
> Thy natural magic and dire property
> On wholesome life usurps immediately.

I pass over the fact that if this is Hamlet's speech his intended dozen or sixteen lines were reduced to six in the course of composition. There are "grounds more relative than this" on which to rest the statement that the lines cannot be his. The moment we assume, as Professor Wilson agrees that we must, the structural coincidence involved in the existence of a play presenting the exact means by which Hamlet's father was murdered, it is manifest that so far as the portrayal of the murder is concerned the important thing is not what the Player-Murderer says but what he does. The murderer has made his entrance, however, and *must say something*. Having this in mind, I cannot imagine more ineffective lines than those which are placed in his mouth. Not only is the poetry of the poorest—as generally throughout what we are permitted to see of the Gonzago-play—but the language used is as vague and general as possible. It is precisely the sort of bombast which we should expect to find in an old play of the sort which

Shakespeare had in mind and at which he took the opportunity to poke a little fun.

Professor Wilson argues that the lines of Lucianus are "but a condensation of the description of the poisoning in the Ghost's speech" and that the words "mixture rank of midnight weeds collected" bring back to the vision of Claudius "in dreadful detail that scene four months before when he too was bending over a sleeping king, about to poison him with 'cursed hebona in a vial.' " Such an argument surely verges on the absurd. When Claudius saw a reproduction of the very method (certainly not a usual one in any age) by which he had poisoned his predecessor, it is not easy to suppose that the ranting lines of the Player-Murderer were required to bring back to his vision the details of the scene enacted four months before. Indeed, since the information received by Hamlet from the Ghost was concerned (with an exception of the first importance to be noticed later) with what had been done rather than with what had been said at the time the murder was committed, any attempt to enlarge or rewrite the speech assigned to Lucianus would necessarily have involved the risk of emphasizing differences rather than likenesses and thus of diminishing the effect of the scene on Claudius. If, however, Hamlet had arrived at an opposite opinion and had decided to rewrite the speech, can there be any doubt that he would have been as concrete as possible? Can there be any doubt, for instance, that instead of referring vaguely to "midnight weeds" (I suppose there are several varieties of midnight weeds from which poisons may be compounded) he would have been careful to mention hebona, which was the poison actually administered? No! No! Even if Hamlet had been so foolish as to think that the impression of the play murder on Claudius would be enhanced by a speech, he could not have been guilty of the malevolent platitudes which fall from the lips of Lucianus.

An equally strong case may be made out against the passage in which the Player-King prophesies to the Player-Queen that she will break her promise not to contract a second marriage after his death. Now we are nowhere told that Gertrude had made any such promise to King Hamlet. If she had, her breach of it must be reckoned as the least of her misdeeds. She had (as Professor Wilson thinks and as I think) committed adultery with Claudius. In marrying her deceased husband's brother she had also committed what Shakespeare's audience clearly understood to be incest. Even in the hysterical violence of the closet scene Hamlet, though he talks about marriage vows, says nothing about the making of a promise to his father not to remarry.

But what is much more important, if the lines under consideration were composed by Hamlet, they must be understood as an attempt to catch the conscience of Gertrude rather than that of Claudius. We know, however, from Hamlet's own words in the "rogue and peasant slave" soliloquy that his intention was otherwise. Like Gertrude, the King was guilty of adultery and incest. In addition he had murdered his brother and his sovereign and had usurped the throne. In the light of this record it can hardly be supposed that Hamlet expected his guilt to unkennel itself merely because he was reminded, however forcibly, that the Queen, in addition to her other misdemeanors, had violated a promise about remarrying which she had made to her first husband.

What, then, are we to conclude: that Shakespeare forgot about Hamlet's inserted speech or did not trouble himself to write it because he was sure that the audience would not notice its omission?—that Hamlet abandoned his plan and did not set down the lines which he had in mind?—that the speech is to be found in some passage in the Gonzago-play other than those to which reference has been made?—or that, for some reason, the speech which Hamlet prepared was never delivered? I am content to rest my case against the first of these alternatives on the statement of Professor Wilson (though his opinion is expressed in a connection slightly different from the present one) that Shakespeare was not "a bungler, a slipshod dramatist, who [left] loose ends and banal obscurities thickly scattered over the central scene of his most famous drama." A conclusive answer to the second alternative is that the dialogue between Hamlet and Horatio shows that the inserted speech had actually been prepared and was ready for delivery a few moments before the performance of the Gonzago-play began. As to the third alternative, it is enough to say that three centuries of criticism have failed to identify Hamlet's speech with any passage in the text other than those which have already been discussed.[2] Before disposing of the final alternative it becomes necessary to say a few words about the posture in which Hamlet stood toward the other persons in the drama and about the practical difficulties with which he was confronted.

Dr. A. C. Bradley, who seems to me the soundest of all Shakespearean critics, has discussed at some length what may be described as the "external theory" of the cause of Hamlet's delay. As Dr. Bradley summarizes the arguments by which this theory is supported, it may be asked what Hamlet was to do "when the Ghost had left him with its commission of vengeance. The King was surrounded not merely by courtiers but by a Swiss body-guard; how was Hamlet to get at him? Was he then to accuse him publicly of the murder? If he did, what would happen? How would he prove the charge? All that he had to offer in proof was—a ghost-story! . . . Obviously, then, even if the court had been

[2] An exception must be noted in the person of Professor J. Q. Adams, who appears to think that Hamlet wrote the entire scene which was presented before the King. I cannot resist the comment that if this be so he certainly talked much better than he wrote.

honest, instead of subservient and corrupt, it would have voted Hamlet mad, or worse, and would have shut him up out of harm's way." While Dr. Bradley regards considerations such as these as insufficient explanations of Hamlet's behavior, and therefore concludes that the external theory will not hold water, he admits that it is "quite probable that, when Hamlet was 'thinking too precisely on the event,' he was considering, among other things, the question how he could avenge his father without sacrificing his own life or freedom," and that "assuredly, also, he was anxious that his act of vengeance should not be misconstrued, and would never have been content to leave a 'wounded name' behind him."

I fully agree that Hamlet's delay was not caused "merely, or mainly, or even to any considerable extent" by external difficulties, but it seems to me that the points admitted by Dr. Bradley are to some extent understated. It was surely not "thinking too precisely on the event" for Hamlet to realize that in order to justify the blow by which Claudius was to be struck down it was essential to denounce him before the whole court. Only three persons—Claudius, Hamlet, and Horatio, to whom Hamlet had recounted the tale unfolded by the Ghost—knew the method by which the late King had been murdered, or knew indeed that he had been murdered at all. If, therefore, the behavior of Claudius were such as to satisfy both Hamlet and Horatio of his guilt, it was certain that the inference of guilt would be drawn by nobody else. The plot of the Gonzago-play made it a perfect instrument to serve notice on the King that Hamlet had discovered his guilt, but as an instrument of public accusation it was entirely worthless. In order to make it serve the latter purpose something had to be added, not for the benefit of the King but for the benefit of the court. Until this something was added, until the King was openly accused of murder, Hamlet could strike only at the peril of his own life and reputation. If we are to take him at his own words, he did not set his life "at a pin's fee," but he valued his reputation so highly that he charged Horatio with his dying breath to "report [his] cause aright to the unsatisfied."

Professor Wilson has not overlooked the force of at least a part of what has just been said. In his opinion it may be taken for granted that "if the interlude proved the Ghost honest Hamlet intended to finish his uncle off immediately afterwards," but he nevertheless pauses to inquire what reason Hamlet was to give the world for the assassination. He calls attention in a footnote to the suggestion of a friendly critic that the suspicions of the courtiers would be aroused by the fact that the scene of the play murder is laid in a garden and that Hamlet's father was known to have died in a garden, but dismisses the suggestion with the apt remark that to accept it "is surely to find Scotland Yard at Elsinore." His own solution of the difficulty is that by a sudden afterthought Hamlet intended the Gonzago-play to have two meanings. To the guilty Claudius the Player-King was of course to represent the murdered King Hamlet, and Lucianus, the Player-Murderer, was to represent himself. On the other hand to the court the Player-King was to represent Claudius and Lucianus was to represent Hamlet. In this way, says Professor Wilson, Hamlet "uses the play to threaten his uncle" and to "prepare the court for the execution to follow."

I am bound to say that this theory seems to me a very strange one. No support whatever is to be found for it in the text. Professor Wilson makes much of the fact that upon the entrance of Lucianus Hamlet describes him as "nephew to the king," and argues that the purpose of Hamlet's remark was to identify himself with Lucianus in the minds of the audience. But what reason is there to doubt that in the original Gonzago-play Lucianus was actually nephew to the King? The plot of Shakespeare's drama had already required him to present to his audience the extraordinary coincidence of an existing play in which a sleeping king was murdered by poison administered through the ears and in which the murderer got the love of the King's wife. Nothing was to be gained and something was to be lost by insisting on the further coincidence involved in making the murderer brother to the King. Doubtless it was on this account that Shakespeare caused Hamlet to tell us in his soliloquy that the players were to present "something like" the murder of his father, and in his conversation with Horatio to say that one scene in the play came "near the circumstance" of his father's death. If Lucianus had been brother to the King in the Gonzago-play, the circumstance of the death of King Hamlet would have been exactly reproduced and the improbability of the entire situation would have been needlessly emphasized.

But a much graver objection to Professor Wilson's theory becomes apparent when we inquire what possible motive Hamlet could have had in seeking to be associated in the minds of the courtiers with the villain of the Gonzago-play. "The Ghost's commands," says Professor Wilson, "the salvation of Gertrude, the family honor of the House of Denmark, forbade any disclosure of the truth. The real meaning of the Gonzago story, the King's meaning, could not be revealed, because the Queen herself was involved. Hamlet was, therefore, obliged to furnish the court with some theory which would explain the Gonzago-play, account for the open discomfiture of his uncle which he hoped it would effect, and justify (*or at any rate make explicable*) the assassination that was to come after. His own rights (i.e., his rights to the throne as his father's son and heir) gave him everything he required."

The weakness of this argument is implicit in the words in parentheses which I have placed in italics. Hamlet could not hope to justify (and surely did not wish to make explicable) an attack on the person of the King by presenting himself to the court in the guise of a cowardly and treacherous assassin about to poison his lawful sovereign. To do so would have been deliberately to misreport his cause to the unsatisfied. Moreover, in charging Claudius with murder Hamlet was not required to involve the Queen in any way. There was no necessity for revealing her adultery, and apart from adultery her only fault had been her "o'er hasty" and incestuous second marriage. As Hamlet's comments on the dialogue between the Player-King and Player-Queen show clearly enough, he had no scruples about calling attention to this fault in public.

It follows from what has been said that while I agree with Professor Wilson that if Hamlet struck the King down, he was under the necessity of giving the world a reason for his act, I find myself strongly in disagreement with the view that the reason which he intended to give was other than the true one—namely, that the King was the murderer of his father. I believe, in short, that in the Gonzago-play the Player-King was to be identified for all purposes with King Hamlet and Lucianus with Claudius, and that at least one of the difficulties with which Hamlet was confronted was to make these identifications as clear to the courtiers as they were likely to be to his uncle.

With the foregoing considerations in mind, we may now proceed to an examination of the last of the alternatives propounded—namely, that the inserted speech was never delivered. So far as I know, only three critics have discussed this possibility. Dr. Furnivall, as quoted in Dr. Furness's note, holds "very strongly that Lucianus's speech is not the [inserted] speech, and that, in fact, the speech is not in the printed play. Either the King's conscience was more quickly stung than Hamlet anticipated, and so the written speech was never needed; or . . . Shakespeare contented himself with showing us . . . that Hamlet altered the play and put his 'dozen or sixteen lines' into action instead of words." Mr. Malleson, also quoted by Dr. Furness, says that if the King had not blenched, "we should have had probably the rest of the dozen lines, which might have contained a hint of the Poisoner's next aim, the seduction to a second marriage of the seeming-virtuous Queen." Dr. Bradley, evidently sharing Mr. Malleson's view that the lines of Lucianus constituted only the first half of the inserted speech, feels that "Hamlet's device proves a triumph far more complete than he had dared to expect. He had thought the King might 'blench,' but he does much more. When only six of the 'dozen or sixteen lines' have been spoken he starts to his feet and rushes from the hall, followed by the whole dismayed Court." I cannot bring myself to believe that Hamlet was the author of any of the wretched lines delivered by Lucianus. Nevertheless, the comments of Mr. Malleson and Dr. Bradley do justice to one of the realities of the situation. When the play was interrupted Lucianus was in the center of the stage. If no interruption had occurred he would (at the least) have had to make his exit, and, as in the case of his entrance, *he would have had to say something.* It is certain, therefore, that his speech was not at an end when the King rose.

It will be observed that only Mr. Malleson has ventured to conjecture what the unspoken lines would probably have contained. In his opinion they "might have contained a hint of the Poisoner's next aim, the seduction to a second marriage of the seeming-virtuous Queen." The suggestion is an acute one, which, in my view of the matter, just misses the mark. The dumb show had already made it clear that the Poisoner was to get the love of his victim's wife and the dialogue between the Player-King and Player-Queen had been full of references to second marriages. In view of the situation existing in Elsinore, these references must have seemed to the courtiers in exceedingly bad taste. They could not, however, standing alone, have been understood as an accusation of murder directed against Claudius.

I am persuaded that the key to the solution of the entire problem is contained in the observation already made that, *with a single exception*, the tale unfolded by the Ghost had been concerned with things done rather than with things said at the time of King Hamlet's death. The exception is to be found in these lines of the Ghost:

> 'Tis *given out*, that sleeping in my orchard,
> *A serpent stung me*, so the whole ear of Denmark
> Is by a forgéd process of my death
> Rankly abused.

Now I think I need not labor an argument in order to show that the Queen was not guilty of complicity in her husband's death. She stands acquitted by the almost unanimous voice of competent criticism. There is not a word in the text to imply, however remotely, that Claudius acted with any other accomplice. It follows that the cause of death must have been "given out" by Claudius. Under circumstances which we can only conjecture he must have said to the Queen, or said to someone, that *King Hamlet had died from the sting of a serpent. The courtiers knew, of course, the cause of death which had been given out; what they did not know was that the process of the death was forged.*

Let us return now to the Gonzago-play and to the necessity for converting it from a secret into an open denunciation of Claudius. My conclusion is that when Claudius rose he prevented the delivery of Hamlet's inserted lines, which were to be spoken by Lucianus either in a soliloquy or in a scene with the Player-Queen. In the former case the lines would have disclosed the intention of the murderer to ascribe the death of his victim to the sting of a serpent. In the latter case the forged process of the death would have been presented directly to the Player-Queen. In either case the effect on the court would have been positively electrifying. The murder of a

King in a garden had been depicted. There had been unseemly talk about second marriages. The extraordinary behavior of Hamlet must have impressed the courtiers that something important was about to take place. The moment Lucianus referred to the sting of a serpent the purport of the Gonzago-play would have been as clear as crystal to everyone in the room. Moreover, the impact of the scene on Claudius would have been doubled. He would have known at once that no attempt to control himself and to brazen matters out could save him. Hamlet not only knew of his guilt but was about to denounce him publicly.

It will no doubt be said that there is no basis in the text for the theory which has just been expounded. I do not agree with any such statement. The last line of Hamlet before the interruption of the play is an attempt to direct the attention of both Claudius and the court to what is about to happen: "You shall see anon how the murderer gets the love of Gonzago's wife." But Claudius has already seen and heard enough and rises in confusion. Hamlet immediately says, "What! frighted with false fire?" There is not a single note on this line in the Furness Variorum edition of *Hamlet*. To me its import is exceedingly plain—*Claudius had been frighted with false fire because the real fire was about to come.*

One other possible objection ought to be noticed. How, it may be argued, if the purposes of Hamlet in the play scene partially miscarried, do we find him in almost hysterical high spirits when conversing with Horatio immediately after the play had been interrupted? I can do no more than to state my answer to this objection. The first purpose of the Gonzago-play had been brilliantly accomplished. The guilt of the King was apparent to both Hamlet and Horatio, and any possibility of doubting the Ghost's word was at an end. I agree with Dr. Bradley that Hamlet's doubt on this point had never been a "genuine doubt" but was rather "an unconscious fiction, an excuse for his delay—and for its continuance." The second purpose of the Gonzago-play—the public accusation of the King—had failed, not because of any weakness on Hamlet's part but because the King had been frighted by false fire. Because it failed—because the King had rushed from the room—Hamlet had been reprieved from the necessity of acting. The high spirits which possessed him in the scene with Horatio were equally compounded of triumph at the discomfiture of the King and relief that he had not been compelled to strike. But I am aware that this argument can only be suggested. To make it good would require an analysis of the character of Hamlet. The subject is a large one, and perhaps too much about it has been written already.

XI
DIVERSITIES OF GIFTS

Now there are diversities of gifts, but the same Spirit
I Corinthians 12.4

1

More than a century ago an Irish priest was appointed rector of St. Mary's Church, which stood then, as it stands today, at the corner of Prince and Vine streets, one square to the south of King Street. St. James Episcopal Church is situated at the corner of Duke and Orange streets, an equal distance to the north of King Street. When the appointment of the priest of St. Mary's was only four years old, the vestry of St. James called to its pulpit a young man who had begun as a lawyer a career which he was destined to end as a bishop. At almost the same time a new minister came to Trinity Lutheran Church, whose lofty spire has overlooked King Street from the south since the concluding decades of the eighteenth century.

They became fast friends. The priest was an ardent Democrat. The Lutheran minister was a Whig. The Episcopal rector regarded parties—"faction," as George Washington would have expressed it—as the besetting sin of Church and State. In spite of these political differences all three were elected to the school board. When President Zachary Taylor died in office, the board met in the Court House in order to pass resolutions of respect. At the close of the meeting the three friends walked, arm in arm, to Trinity Church in order to take part in a religious service in memory of the dead President. The picture which they presented was never forgotten by those who saw it, and has become for us on King Street a symbol of not the least part of the contribution which America has made to the wisdom and charity of the world.

But indeed the precedents which make for tolerance among us run back much further than a century. A decade before the last of the witches was hanged in Salem, the "Great Law" of William Penn had provided that no person who acknowledged one Almighty God to be the creator and ruler of the world, and who professed himself obliged in conscience to live peaceably and justly under the civil government, should in any wise be molested or prejudiced by reason of his conscientious persuasion or practice. Relying on this assurance, several families from the Palatinate, descendants of the distressed Swiss Mennonites, settled on the Pequea Creek, whereupon Penn sent to the Conestoga Indians a present—consisting, somewhat inappropriately, of powder and shot—and a message requiring their friendship to "the Palatines, settled near Pequae." The Indians made a conciliatory reply, and in the course of a few years the Mennonites were followed by coreligionists of Penn himself; by Amish, called in early days Beardy Men and Hooker Mennonites—the latter because of the hooks and eyes which they still use on their clothes instead of buttons; by Dunkers or Tunkers, with beards as long as those of the Amish, but without the distinguishing hooks and eyes; by Moravians, who founded a congregation of which Count Zinzendorf is reckoned as the first pastor; and by one Conrad Beissel, who lived first as a hermit on the banks of the Cocalico and afterwards founded a monastic society whose members attained such excellence in music as to be publicly rewarded by the King of England, and such skill in printing as to be chosen printers of money for the Continental Congress.

If to these little-known sectarians, referred to locally by the collective designation of "plain people," there be added representatives of the usual Protestant denominations and the Catholics who laid the foundations of St. Mary's—the women mixing the mortar while the men gathered the stones from the adjoining farms—it is not hard to credit the statement of an authority on the subject that a pedestrian on King Street may meet representatives of as many as thirty sects during the course of a walk on that thoroughfare.

2

He who would see the plain people of the present generation can make no better beginning than by following King Street to our market house on any market day. The land on which we are standing was set apart in 1730 "for the erection of a market within the town" and has ever since served its appointed purpose, the stalls in the market house being rented annually by the city to the highest bidders at a public auction.

Here is a placid Mennonite housewife who, with the help of her little daughter, is selling vegetables raised on her husband's farm, and in addition a variety of products of her own handiwork—yellow noodles for "schmaltzing" (baking with bread crumbs) or making soup, pickled pigs' feet called "souse," dried apples or "schnitz," "schmierkaes," and thick sugar cookies which are known as "pepper nuts." If the time of the year were near Shrove Tuesday, her wares would also include "fasnachts"—raised doughnuts without holes—which are eaten on that feast day.

Being indoors now, she has removed the black bonnet, shaped like a short pokebonnet, in which she came to market, and in so doing has uncovered a small white cap resembling a miniature sunbonnet, the strings of which are tied under her chin. She wears a black garb (it might also be gray or, indeed, any quiet print) consisting of a waist buttoned close to the neck, but without a collar, and a long full skirt. A cape made of the same material as the dress completes as plain a costume as may well be imagined. It is curious, nevertheless, to observe the universality of the experience that the effort to avoid distinction in dress inevitably defeats its purpose. In a somewhat similar connection the Quakers, in attempting to abolish ritual, have unwittingly created an exceedingly effective ritual out of silence.

The little girl does not wear a garb. She has not yet renounced the world and joined the church—has not "come out" and "given herself up," as the Mennonites themselves express it. She will make her own decision on that point when she has arrived at years of discretion. Perhaps she will never give herself up, and unless she does so she will continue to dress as her own taste and that of her mother determine. If, in due time, she concludes to take the momentous step, she will appear some morning attired like her mother, and from that day forward the vanity of personal adornment will be a thing of the past.

If her father had come to market it might be possible to tell whether the family belongs to the Old Mennonites, who are the more numerous and the less rigid, or to the New Mennonites, who claim to have returned to an earlier and more excellent standard. Among the former, the wearing of beards is optional; among the latter, beards are considered productive of both pride and envy, and are consequently forbidden. A Mennonite with a beard is, therefore, certainly an Old Mennonite, but one without a beard may belong to either of the two branches of the church. Old Mennonites vote at elections and are allowed to hold such public offices as school director and road supervisor, but not to be members of the legislature. Their ministers are expected not to vote. New Mennonites do not vote at all. If one of them becomes a backslider in the eyes of the church, the other members of his own family are not allowed to eat at the same table with him, and his wife withdraws from him.

Old Mennonite ministers are chosen in the following manner. When a vacancy occurs and a new appointment is required, several men go into a small room and receive privately oral nominations to fill the vacancy. After this has been done, an opportunity is given to any nominee to excuse himself from the service. Those who are not excused, if, for instance, six in number, are brought before six Bibles, in one of which a lot has been placed. Each candidate takes up a book, and the one within whose book the lot is found is the chosen minister.

3

Across the aisle of the market a portly Amishman, his hollow-chested wife, and their little son are engaged in selling poultry and potatoes. The rule among the Amish requires that the men shave their upper lips and allow their beards to grow, whence, as already stated, they were formerly known as Beardy Men—a name which went out of use when the wearing of beards became generally fashionable during the period of the Civil War. Our Amishman has kept the rule to the letter, and his beard, which is reddish brown in color, is a full and noble one. Except for the necessary absence of a beard, the little boy is a perfect manikin. His hair, like that of his father, has been cut straight over the forehead and hangs almost to his shoulders, and he wears the characteristic Amish garb consisting of a dark coat and waistcoat fastened with hooks and eyes, long trousers (which are worn without suspenders), and a round-crowned black felt hat with an extremely wide brim. Though he may not know it, the hooks and eyes on his clothing are symbols of an inherited pacifism and express the abhorrence which his ancestors felt for the brass buttons which have always played such conspicuous parts in adorning the uniform of a soldier.

The Amish mother, though she too wears a garb, is much less restricted in her choice of colors than her Mennonite neighbor. Her bonnet—which has a long visor hiding her face and a "curtain" reaching to her shoulders—and the folded shawl or handkerchief meeting demurely over her breast are black, but her closely fitting dress is a dull magenta and the apron which she wears over it is royal blue. She has selected these colors, not because she mistakenly believes them to be inconspicuous, but because she regards them as "unworldly"—that is, not in general use. Certain shades of green and purple, as well as magenta and royal blue, appear to have been definitely approved by her coreligionists as unworldly colors. The implications of this approval are not altogether unnoticed by the world itself. A merchant on King Street once told me of a customer of his who hesitated about buying a piece of cloth which was otherwise acceptable to her on the ground that the color "looked Amish." He hastened to assure her that she was mistaken, and she completed the purchase.

The Amish love of color is not limited in its expression to the dress of the women. Houses and barns are sometimes gayly painted. A blue gate is said, though perhaps incorrectly, to be a sign that a marriageable daughter is to be found within. Before the days of automobiles every Amish family possessed a wagon covered with yellow oilcloth. These wagons were built without dashboards and usually without whip sockets—the latter being regarded, except among one faction of the Amish, as symbolical of compulsion or force. Some members of the church now drive automobiles, but this practice is strongly disapproved by others.

One becomes a member of the Mennonite Church by conversion, but one is born into the Amish communion. There are less than twenty family names in the entire fellowship, and I have never heard of an Amish convert. On the other hand, instances of voluntary withdrawal from the church are exceedingly rare. The small number of surnames sometimes creates difficulties. A public-school teacher with whom I was acquainted was elected to teach at an ungraded country school having thirty-four pupils, all but two of whom were named Stoltzfus. In order to avoid confusion it became necessary to invoke medieval precedents, and to speak of "Hickory John" and "Black Isaac." A client of mine prefixed the word "Spring" to his given name because of a large spring which was located on his farm, and invariably signed his name in its revised form to checks and legal documents.

Though in nearly all connections the Amish have been content to accept the views and continue the practices which have been handed down to them, it by no means follows that they are lacking in natural spirit and gayety. Indeed, their young men sometimes display a wildness of behavior which seems altogether out of keeping with the soberness of their appearance. Time out of mind they have had a passionate interest in fast and spirited horses. In spite of a traditional adherence to the Republican Party, which originally resulted from their opinions on the subject of slavery, they voted the Democratic ticket in the presidential election of 1932 because of their deep-seated hostility to national prohibition. At wedding parties, called "infares," the revelry frequently continues all night. On these occasions both young and old join in a game not unlike "Hunt the Slipper," which is played with what is known as a "bloom-sock"—a handkerchief or towel, twisted and doubled, with the ends tied in a knot. In the course of the game the bloom-sock is passed secretly from hand to hand in order to confuse that one of the players whose obligation it is to find it. As opportunity offers, the other players hit him with the bloom-sock. If he is able to seize it, his obligation is discharged and another takes his place.

4

You may well suppose at first glance that the man in charge of the next market stall is also an Amishman. A second glance, however, will serve to correct your mistake. His shaven upper lip and full beard are suggestive of the Amish practice, but his gray coat of clerical cut is both lighter in color and finer in material than that of any Amishman. Most of all, the large buttons with which his coat is fastened show conclusively that he belongs to some other denomination. As a matter of fact, both beard and garb result from his own choice and are not rendered obligatory by the discipline of his church. He is one of the Dunkers, or, as they prefer to be called, the Brethren. As the commonly accepted name indicates, he believes in "dipping"—that is, in baptism by immersion.

The members of the various "plain" denominations do not greatly differ from one another in theological beliefs. All of them have retained the ordinances of baptism, whether by pouring or immersion, and of the Lord's Supper. Some of them also practise feet-washing.

An eyewitness of a generation ago [1] has described a feet-washing and love feast among the Dunkers. The ceremony was held in the evening and in church, the seats of which were so constructed that by turning down the backs of some of them tables could be formed. At the appointed time the presiding bishop rose in his place and read the account of the feet-washing contained in the Gospel according to Saint John. In front of him stood four men, who, at the words "laid aside his garments," took off their coats, and, at the words "took a towel and girded himself," put on long white aprons tied around the waist. Two of these men washed feet and two wiped, and, having thus ministered, were ministered to by four others who took their places, and who were in turn replaced until all had taken part. The women, who occupied a separate side of the church, performed the same ordinance for themselves in a similar manner. At its conclusion all present

[1] Mrs. Phebe Earle Gibbons, whose essay, "Pennsylvania Dutch," appeared in the *Atlantic Monthly* for October 1869. I have made use of her observations in a number of other places throughout this paper.

partook of a love feast consisting of soup, bread, butter, and meat, without salt or other condiment. When all had eaten, a young bishop rose at the center of the main table, shook hands with the sister on his left, and kissed the brother on his right. From brother to brother and from sister to sister the kiss went around the congregation until the last sister, who had no one to kiss, went forward and kissed the first one with whom the bishop had shaken hands, thus completing the chain of unity. This ceremony was followed by communion, which was administered with bread or cakes, unleavened and sweetened, and home-made wine.

But if theological differences among the plain sectarians are slight and unimportant, there are many differences in customs and practices which rest indirectly on theological grounds, and of which the lawyer who maintains an office on King Street is bound to take notice. All of the plain denominations forbid their members to institute legal proceedings under any circumstances whatever, though both Dunkers and Mennonites are permitted, in extremity and by way of last resort, to defend themselves against unjustified suits and to appeal to the police for protection.

The latter permission, which is not accorded to the Amish, is founded upon a passage in the Acts of the Apostles in which it is narrated that forty Jews entered into a conspiracy to kill Paul. But Paul sent his nephew to the chief captain to inform him of the conspiracy, and the latter put Paul under the charge of soldiers to be brought safe to Felix, the governor. For some reason, however, a Dunker may defend himself in court or ask for protection *only once*. If the verdict goes against him he may not appeal, and if his request for help is unanswered he may not renew it but must take the consequences.

The idea of nonresistance is not entirely confined to human relationships. Among the striking peculiarities of a branch of the Dunker fellowship is a strong opposition to the use of lightning rods. "If," said one of their preachers, "God wishes to preserve the building, he can preserve it without the lightning rod. If he does not wish to preserve it, I am willing to submit to the result."

5

Only a few persons may now be found who claim membership in the monastic society founded by Conrad Beissel. The brothers and sisters wore a habit similar to that of the Capuchins or White Friars and lived in separate houses, sleeping on benches with blocks of wood for pillows and eating with wooden forks from plates made of thin octagonal pieces of poplar board. Even the flagons, goblets, and trays used in the communion service were made of wood. The celibate brothers and sisters met only in religious exercises and at love feasts. Celibacy was recommended, though not enjoined, and no vows with reference to it were taken. The strictest simplicity was practised by all.

On one occasion a brother who had taken the name Onesimus, and who, though designated as prior, was subordinate to Beissel, ordered a bell from Europe without the knowledge of the society and caused to be placed on it a Latin inscription in which his name was included. When the bell arrived it was duly paid for, but a council was held in order to determine what to do with it. The first decision was to break the bell and bury the pieces in the earth. The next morning, however, Beissel appeared before the council and said he had reflected that, as the brothers were poor, the bell should be pardoned. This was accordingly done and the bell was sold. For many years the pardoned bell, still bearing the name of the innovating prior who had caused it to be cast, was used to summon worshipers to Trinity Lutheran Church. Afterwards it passed into the hands of one of the fire companies on King Street.

Though Beissel was surpassed both in education and in native powers of mind by a number of his monastic associates, he was a first-rate musician and composer. He developed an unusual style of singing, founded on the music of nature as found in the tones of the Aeolian harp. The music was set in four, six, and eight parts. All the parts save the bass were led and sung exclusively by women, the men being confined to the bass, which was set in two parts, the high and the low bass. The former, in combination with one of the female parts, is said to have been an excellent imitation of the concert horn, and the latter to have resembled the deep tones of the organ. An early visitor to the monastery reported that the singers scarcely opened their mouths or moved their lips, and added that the effect was to throw the voices up to the ceiling of the chapel, which was not high, so that the tones seemed to be entering from above with almost superhuman softness and devotion.

The commissioners who were sent by the English Government to visit the society after the French and Indian War were so charmed by what they heard that they requested that a copy of the music be sent to the royal family in England. This request was cheerfully complied with. About a year afterwards a box was received, three or four feet long and two or two and a half feet wide, containing a present in return. What the present was is not certainly known—none having seen it but Beissel and one Jaebez, who was then prior and into whose care the box had been consigned. On this occasion Beissel had no afterthoughts. He caused the box and its contents to be buried secretly. From a hint dropped by Jaebez it is supposed that the contents consisted of images of the King and Queen in full costume. Perhaps something may be said in justification of the feeling that it is harder to pardon an image than a bell.

6

The history of religious differences would appear to show that it is harder to pardon a heretic than either an image or a bell. If so, the views of some of Beissel's coreligionists must be regarded as exceptional. "We deny eternal punishment," said one of them. "Those souls who become sensible of God's great goodness and clemency, and acknowledge his lawful authority . . . and that Christ is the only true Son of God, are received into happiness; but those who continue obstinate are kept in darkness until the Great Day, when light will make all happy."

But a belief in universal regeneration has played no appreciable part in the spirit of tolerance which, from those early and vivid days

> When reds and blues were indeed red and blue,

has always manifested itself on King Street. For tolerance, as I have tried to show elsewhere, is a by-product of democracy, and though rooted in the greatest of the divine virtues, must be reckoned as a civil virtue rather than as an ecclesiastical one. It does not result from theological views about human regeneration. Still less does it depend upon the acceptance of that curious modern point of view which regards a judicial attitude as one by which judgment is withheld rather than given. Its practice is summed up for us on King Street in the memory of a priest and two ministers who thought themselves the better citizens and not the worse churchmen because they were willing to attend a religious ceremony in a Protestant church in order to do honor to the memory of a President of the United States.

XII

A LETTER TO MY FATHER

DEAR FATHER:

I am not sure whether or not you ever read Kipling's *Jungle Book*. If you did so it must have been long ago, when the *Jungle Book* was first published and was read aloud to me as a very small boy, a little at a time, just before we were called to supper on winter evenings. In that case I think you will remember how Tabaqui, the jackal, came for no good purpose to the cave of Father and Mother Wolf and, having made a meal on some bones which they had thrown aside, embarrassed them by telling them how beautiful their children were. As Kipling points out, they were quite properly embarrassed, because there is nothing so unlucky as to compliment children to their faces.

Perhaps it is also unlucky to compliment the old to their faces, but if there is such a precept I do not think that it applies to the dead. I may, therefore, write words now without embarrassment to either of us, which I never spoke, and indeed would not have wished to speak, in times past. If it seems strange to you that in the course of what follows I refer to you chiefly in the past tense, you must set it down to the literary affectation by which we are accustomed to speak and write of the dead in that way.

By a necessity even more compelling—a necessity which, in the very nature of the case, enters into every human relationship—I can think of you only in the form in which I knew you. You were over forty years of age when you were married, and though you lived to see me grow from childhood to be as old as you were on your wedding day, I saw you—at first through the mistaken eyes of childhood, but at last in very truth—always as an old man. So it comes about that in the picture of you that I like best only your eyes are young. You wear a sedate overcoat, hanging loosely from a buttoned top button, and a sedate felt hat. Your beard is not the full and splendid one which you first grew in the year of the Centennial—when, having cut yourself in shaving, you came to the quiet resolution that it would be a long time before you shaved again—but is close-clipped and gray. You stand so straight as to seem to lean backward a little, but your step has lost the spring which made you delight, in your youth, in hunting and fishing for trout, and with which in the days of my own boyhood you set the pace of our Sunday walks together.

"Where shall we walk today?" I would say on each succeeding Sunday, being, like Caesar's Gauls, desirous of new things. "Do you see that barn out there?" you would invariably reply, and we would make the accustomed circuit that took us by the barn, talking on many subjects, but chiefly of the ancient history which I was studying at school and of that other history which you had seen with your eyes in the making.

It would be easy to enumerate here the great events to which you were a witness—how you saw three of the five great wars in which our country has been engaged, the first telegraph, the first telephone, the first (and perhaps almost the last) trolley car, the first aeroplane, the first radio, the discovery of the North and South Poles, and a thousand other events of like moment and significance. But the truth is that you were in general very little influenced by objective events. Indeed, apart from purely personal happenings I can think of only two occurrences in the course of your whole life by which you were greatly affected—the Civil War, and the publication of the works of Emerson.

The Civil War irrevocably fixed your politics. You were born and brought up along the Susquehanna River in the exciting days of the underground railroad. You have told me how a boyhood playmate of yours was charged on a certain day to stay away from the haymow. Boylike, he went there at the first opportunity, and on poking about at random with a fork was startled by a cry of terror from a "black man" —the phrase which you always used—who was hidden under the hay. Doubtless little boys were impressed by such experiences and came to more or less unconscious conclusions about them. You have told me, too, that your father was a Whig who could not quite bring himself to vote for Frémont, and that, four years later, after watching a torchlight parade of some followers of Douglas, you burst into the room where he was sitting, demanding passionately, "Who are we for?" "We are for Lincoln," your father answered slowly, and you went away satisfied. Two years later you read about the fight between the *Monitor* and the *Merrimac* in Hampton Roads, and made a boy's model of the *Monitor* which stands beside me as I write. Later still you watched Lee's cavalry riding down the west bank of the river before the battle opened at Gettysburg, while the smoke from the burning bridge at Columbia darkened the sky.

From such experiences as these came your whole-hearted devotion and loyalty to the Republican Party, which are somehow summed up for me as from a bygone age in the "Battle Hymn of the Republic" and which, though a Republican, I do not share, and a sort of mystical faith in political equality—"the right," as you used to say, "of bad or ignorant men to express their badness or ignorance at the polls"—which I also do not share, but which was doubtless the best element in what seems to me to have been the generally bad business of reconstruction. Perhaps I fail to do full justice to this latter feeling. If so the reason is that I never fully understood it. You were sometimes inclined to leave gaps in your expression of abstract ideas.

There was nothing abstract about your love of Emerson. You planned in your youth to go on a walking trip to Concord in order to see him, but for some reason which I do not know the plan came to nothing, and as a result you never saw him in the flesh. But you read and pondered every word of his prose and verse, and you reread the essays every year of your life with what seemed a growing sense of their majesty and power. A month or two before you died you asked me to have rebound the two volumes that you cherished most (Emerson's *Prose Works*, James R. Osgood and Company, Boston, 1876), saying that you wanted me to have them as my inheritance from you. They stand on my bookshelves now. I do not count them the richest part of my inheritance, but I want you to know that I do not undervalue them.

I shall never forget a night, ten or a dozen years ago, when Professor Bliss Perry, speaking under the auspices of the chapter of the Phi Beta Kappa Society at the college in the city in which we lived, chose Emerson as the subject of his address. The speaker told of Emerson's early life and mentioned the death of his first wife and of his two brilliant brothers. "But," said Professor Perry, speaking after a little pause with a sort of ringing suavity of utterance, "he had pulled himself together, being of the old unbeatable Puritan stuff; he had married again, had bought a house, had published a little book, had backed himself to win against his generation—against the world." I remember nothing else about that address, except that the speaker succeeded in expressing a part of your own love and admiration for your hero. When it was over, your face was quite pink and radiant behind your beard, and your rather small brown eyes were bright with unwonted excitement. I asked you whether you wanted to join those of the audience who were going forward to shake hands with Professor Perry, but you shook your head. You were never a ready speaker and you knew that it would have been useless to try to put into words the delight which the evening had given you. If Professor Perry ever sees these words, he will know that for at least one auditor he made a perfect speech that night.

My own feeling about Emerson has always been that there was in him a sort of superficial optimism which arose from ignoring or denying some of the obvious facts of life. Then I think about you—how you lived and how you died—and I am not so sure.

But all that I have written is beside the point of what I really meant to tell you. You are going to be remembered here on earth for a very much longer time than you would have thought possible, if, indeed, you had thought about that subject at all. I shall tell you why. There is a feeling abroad about you which has been growing in the years which have passed since your death. I have seen it in the face of Herman, the gravedigger—who, in the intervals between the demands of his calling, was accustomed to help you in the garden and in making your grape wine—and in the faces of neighbors and tradespeople who knew and spoke with you during your later years. I have heard of it from the lips of the men who worked for you in the prime of your life on the Elizabeth Farms where I was born. I have heard of it, too, from the lips of those men's sons, who never knew you and who will perhaps speak of it to their sons in after days. This feeling is that you were a very wise man. I think it is true. I write deliberately—I think you were the wisest man I ever knew.

There are many kinds of wisdom. There is the broken but triumphant wisdom of the twice-born, about which you knew nothing whatever. There is the sudden and bewitched wisdom of insight, which belongs to poets and Celts and about which you—who, to use Santayana's wistful phrase, were "almost a poet"—knew something. But there is another sort of wisdom, which was the greater part of yours, founded on patience and simplicity and on watching

> the certain things,
> Swine, and slow moons like silver rings,
> And the ripening of the plums.

It was an unconscious wisdom on your part. I remember asking you once—half shyly, because I was almost sure in advance what your answer would be—whether you thought you had learned anything in the course of your lifetime about the mystery of life. You answered, as I had expected, that you had learned nothing at all. And yet, though you were unaware of the fact itself, it is easy enough to set down some of the sources of your wisdom and some of the things in which it consisted.

I have said that it was founded on simplicity and on the things of earth. You were brought up as a nurseryman, and you spent the happiest years of your life as the manager of more than a thousand acres of farm land. Though you came afterward to live in the city, the house which you chose on King Street was at the city's very edge. You lived there for a generation without taking more than a casual interest in civic affairs and without playing any active part in them. You were somewhat skeptical about what most Americans regard as progress. You were never a leader. Confident and successful men respected you and went their ways. I am not sure you were sorry to see them go. You were not readily impressed by the reputation of success.

At heart you were always a farmer. I do not remember having ever heard you use the word "nature," and it may well be that you would have sympathized with Meredith's caustic reference to "birds and beasts and herbs which ninnies call nature in books." But your interest in individual birds and beasts and herbs was unfailing. I do not think that you could have brought yourself to live anywhere without a garden in which to renew your youth by budding and grafting trees, to grow, among other vegetables, the tomatoes of which you were so proud, and to set up some of the red-and-green wren houses which you made not only for yourself but for half the children of the neighborhood. To the end of your life you found comfort in sitting alone for long hours out of doors. Stevenson has called attention somewhere to the characteristic simplicity of old soldiers and old priests. The comment is acutely made, but it seems to me that he should have added old farmers to his enumeration. The reason for all these simplicities is the same—lifelong adherence to a code which, whatever theories may be, actually works in practice. We are all withdrawals from the earth and in the end she never disappoints us.

No one knew you well who had not heard you speak at one time or another of your way of life on the Elizabeth Farms—of your mare, Nellie, on whose back you rode over the red fields and along the little streams that flow between the hills, and of how, pausing sometimes in the hush of early spring, great thoughts would come to you which you could never quite put into words; of Peter and Annie, the middle-aged couple who kept house for you; of the annual adventures of sowing and reaping; and of the sick animals to whom, for want of a veterinary, you ministered at need. Your successes in this latter connection seemed to give you greater pleasure than any others which came to you. You would tell, in a vein of ingenuous boasting which was otherwise quite foreign to you, how you studied the few medical works which were available in order to interpret the symptoms from which a given patient was suffering, and how, after due deliberation, you decided to prescribe such and such a medication. Then would come a narration of how the medicine was administered, and finally a celebration of the results accomplished. "Jolly!" you would say proudly. "When I went to the stable in the morning anyone could see that that mule was going to get well."

Less often you spoke of the people of that entire countryside—descendants, most of them, of Hessian prisoners of the Revolutionary War—who came to consult you in all the vicissitudes of their lives. I do not say that it is so, but if you were inclined to overestimate your skill and address with animals, you greatly underestimated your influence on the men and women who, in a not very different fashion, were committed to your care. It so happens that I have met few of those people face to face. One of them, who was a child when she knew you, said recently to someone, who repeated the saying to me, that when she felt like punishing her children she always stopped and asked herself what you would think about it. Another of them, who is now an old man, came to see me a month or two ago, bringing with him a letter which you had written him when you were over eighty years of age. He had seen you only once or twice in more than forty years. He thought that I should like to see what you had written and perhaps should like to copy it. The letter itself he would not let me keep. He said he wanted to give it to his son.

The last time you visited Elizabeth in the flesh was even later than the date on which that letter was written. There was to be a reunion of some of the old residents of the neighborhood and you had been asked to make a little speech. We arrived early at the church in which the ceremonies were to be held, and you and I walked alone as far as the bridge over the stream that flows midway between the church and the mansion house. You stood on the bridge, very frail and gray, but erect and unbroken, thinking perhaps on that June afternoon, as Malory thought on a day in May so many years ago, of "old gentleness and old service, and many kind deeds that were forgotten by negligence," and of such other matters to which, it may be conjectured, the thoughts of the very old turn. You called my attention to a fence along one of the fields, which needed to be repaired. "If I were manager of these farms now," you said, "I would say to Peter and John, 'Drop what you are doing for a little while, and let us fix that piece of fence down by the bridge.' " Then you were silent for a long time, evaluating the greater paradox and the less. At last you smiled and said, speaking slowly as your wont was, "In order to do that, all I should have to do would be to get Peter and John out of their graves, and if I were young again I think I could do that."

Though you lacked both the means and the inclination to travel, had never made the four hours' journey by rail which would have taken you to New York, and, indeed, had been only once or twice outside the limits of your own state, you were without exception the least parochially minded man I have ever known, and the one least influenced by classifications and catchwords. You instinctively disbelieved in the existence of

> The Anthropophagi, and men whose heads
> Do grow beneath their shoulders.

If, by some miracle of time and space, you had been set down in the court of the Great Khan, you would not have entertained for a moment that deep-seated human delusion of which even the gifted Greeks were not wholly free, that those who speak an unknown tongue are necessarily barbarians. You would not have reminded yourself that you were a Nordic and that the Khan was of a different race. Setting aside the matter of your personal shyness, of which you had not a little, you would have had no sense of essential superiority or inferiority. You would have met the Khan with perfect simplicity and dignity, and because he was a man you would have known the nature of his hopes and fears and the subjects of his deepest interests.

You used on occasions a ceremonious and stately sort of courtesy which would doubtless have pleased the Khan as much as it sometimes pleased others. A friend of mine has told me of having had a conversation with you on the street, at the conclusion of which he asked you to come to see him and his wife. You answered, "I am an old man and I go out very seldom in the evening, but when I sit at home I think of many delightful things." "Exactly," as my friend said to me, "as if your father sat at home in the evening thinking how delightful it would be to call on Carol and me."

You once sought—I suspect somewhat whimsically—to justify your slowness of speech by saying that you tried never to advance an argument without restating to yourself the truth which you meant to express, as it might be restated from the point of view of your adversary. The whimsicality lay in the fact, which you knew very well, that your slowness of speech was not confined to argumentative matters; but the rule which you laid down is, for all that, the rule of a true liberal. You were a liberal in everything—in your predispositions toward social and economic questions; in your religious views, which, apart from the doctrine of nonresistance in which you did not believe, were strongly similar to those held by the Quakers; in your attitude toward science and scientific research. I remember the interest which you took in the implications of the new physics, and the comment which you made on a book which contained an explanation of the Einstein theory. You read the book twice, and when you had finished it for the second time you said to me, "I did not understand all of this book, but I did understand some of it. I have known all my life that there is only one thing in the world, and the scientists working in their own way are on the track of finding it out." The idea which you expressed is of course as old as Democritus and some of those other Greek philosophers who were half poets, instead of being half scientists, as are the philosophers of today; but I agree with you that in scientific matters the signs of the times are good. If the scientists can keep their verities within five thousand years of the guesses of the poets, they have every reason to be proud.

I have written this much, and yet I have not written what wisdom is or what a man must do or refrain from doing in order to become wise. No man, it seems, may transmit to his son the wisdom that is his. The secret of its attainment is hidden even from himself, and is not to be purchased with money or expected as the certain reward of age and experience or won by taking anxious thought. If it were otherwise, we should all come at last to the full stature of wisdom, and, having done so, we should put away those foolish things whereby we are troubled and made afraid.

"Raphael paints wisdom," said your master Emerson, "Handel sings it, Phidias carves it, Shakespeare writes it, Wren builds it, Columbus sails it. . . ." You, who painted no pictures and carved no statues, whose songs were without notes and whose poems were without words, who built houses only for birds and who never sailed adventuring on any of the Seven Seas, came also to wisdom by a road of your own finding. It was not the road of the gifted and the great of this world. I am mindful, nevertheless, of the saying of the apostle that the foolishness of God is wiser than men.

Perhaps a knowledge of this truth is the greatest of all the blessings which have come to me as

Your Son